The FRENCH WAY *with* DESIGN

The
FRENCH WAY
with DESIGN

MOVING FORWARD WHILE LOOKING BACK

BETTY LOU PHILLIPS

PHOTOGRAPHS BY DAN PIASSICK

GIBBS SMITH
TO ENRICH AND INSPIRE HUMANKIND

First Edition
18 17 16 15 14   5 4 3 2 1

Published by

Gibbs Smith

P.O. Box 667

Layton, Utah 84041

1.800.835.4993 orders

www.gibbs-smith.com

Designed by Rita Sowins
Page Production by Melissa Dymock

Printed and bound in China

Gibbs Smith books are printed on either recycled,
100% post-consumer waste, FSC-certified papers or on
paper produced from sustainable PEFC-certified forest/
controlled wood source. Learn more at www.pefc.org.

Library of Congress Control Number: 2014934846

ISBN 13: 978-1-4236-3506-2

CONTENTS

ACKNOWLEDGMENTS

WHEN IT COMES TO PRODUCING A BOOK, the credits are endless. Many people play a role in its success.

Madge Baird has been my editor *par excellence* for all but the first of my thirteen design books. My gratefulness continues to grow for her expertise and encouragement, which I treasure along with her friendship. In addition, I appreciate the efforts of Rita Sowins, book designer; Melissa Dymock, production editor; Debbie Uribe, editorial assistant; and Marty Lee, production manager. And, of course, I hardly take for granted the endeavors of the Gibbs Smith marketing team, in particular Kim Eddy for assistance with events and signings.

Nor do I take for granted the effort the following designers, architects and contractors put into creating the alluring, satisfying rooms that make up this book: Larry Boerder, Andy Bringardner, Ron Davidson, Ruth Gay, Ken Harbert, Laura Kutcher, Kelly Phillips, Pamela Pierce, John Remington, John Sebastian, Aline Steinbach, Michael Werchek, Meghan Whitworth and Nicole Zarr.

I appreciate, too, the help of those whose educated eyes assisted on photo shoots, especially Rachel Berry, Sharman Keister, Kelly Phillips, Alex Rico, Amy Werntz, Meghan Whitworth and Anah Witter.

As always, I would like to extend a special thank-you to photographer Dan Piassick. His wife, artist Amy Werntz, also helped make our shoots abroad successful.

Carved chairs with cabriole legs and rush seats surround a pedestal table, at which conversation readily flows. After Louis XVI ascended the throne in 1774, he gave the Petit Trianon, formal gardens and all, to Marie Antoinette with the words, "To you who love flowers so, I present this bouquet." With unbending determination, the queen refashioned the gardens, installing a more natural look tailored to her taste.

An eighteenth-century armoire, glazed dove gray, holds a collection of *faïence*, the French name for Faenza—an Italian pottery center that produced painted majolica ware on opaque, pure white earthenware for export as early as the fifteenth century. Readily accessible to enhance the dining experience are pitchers and platters from Neal & Co. and from The Gray Door, both in Houston.

One of the nicest aspects of writing a book is the opportunity to meet and get to know so many interesting people on both sides of the Atlantic Ocean. Special thanks, therefore, goes to those both in the U.S. and abroad who opened the doors to their impressive *bastides* and *maisons*, permitting us to share the architectural splendor that serves as a backdrop for their personal style and creativity.

Also, meriting a warm thank-you: John Adams, Paul Barrett, John Boggess, Ana Bohilla, Donna Burley, Joan Cecil, Jim Dahlgren, Jeffrey Dashley, Joe Demoruelle, Kathy Dimmitt, Allan Duck, Esther Gandal, Christy Gatchell, Carla Huddleston, Will Kolb, Thomas Love, Annick McNally, Patrick McNally, Michael Naoum, Jerry Nogalski, Martin Norkowski, Allan Rodewald, Danny Salazar, Penny Sanders, Janice Stuerzl, Michael Schmidt, Linda Swain, Michelle Toleos, Tom Trovato, Julie Willenbrock and Pete Wilton. Special thanks goes also to Thomas Johnson and Joe Carino, who responded to both late-night and extraordinarily early-morning computer-related calls.

Deserving of thanks is friend extraordinaire Letitia Jett-Guichard, along with her reason-for-living-in-France, Alexander Guichard, and their daughter Andrea Fletcher.

Also, I am indebted to my valued co-workers, designers whose myriad skills I cherish: Laura Kutcher, Kelly Phillips and Meghan Whitworth.

Add to the above list a love and appreciation for my husband and family, whose patience during the process of writing this book has been admirable.

Finally, I express admiration for the French, who excel not only in the art of making decorating look effortless, but also in fusing the past with the present—as their flair was the inspiration for this book.

Unfortunately, it is nearly impossible to replicate the weathered patina of ancient terra-cotta, which literally means "baked earth." Applying a lime wash doesn't generally produce the coveted warmth and character.

INTRODUCTION

THE FRENCH HAVE BEEN A FORCE within the decorating world ever since Louis XIV swung open the gilded gates leading to his father's once-modest hunting lodge—refashioned into the sumptuous Château de Versailles—in the late seventeenth century. Daz-

In nineteenth-century Paris, men known as *pécheurs de lune* searched "by the light of the moon" for junk to sell at stalls set up in the city center—that is, until banished by the police to the capital's outskirts. Some of these markets still exist today, with Clignancourt flea market being the largest.

zled by the splendor of the sprawling palace, aristocrats fixated on the period's class divide, quite naturally clamored for imposing, heroic-proportioned baroque furnishings worthy of the monarchy. Enviable, richly carved throne-like chairs, tables with scrolled legs, opulent textiles and marquetry chests with ornate mounts typified the unabashedly luxe look of *châteaux*, manor houses, villas and mansions, where excessive proof of one's status ruled.

Befitting living areas more unassumingly scaled than the vast, lofty spaces of Versailles, to say nothing of a less pompous way of life, the expertly crafted eighteenth-century furnishings of Louis XV, Louis XIV's great-grandson, exhibited more restraint. Gracious curves, romantic motifs and asymmetrical silhouettes defined the less pretentious rococo movement. As *salons*—social gatherings of prominent, intellectually minded Parisians—became *de rigueur*, the privileged class sought comfortable, easily movable furnishings conducive to the art of conversation. This gave

Tailored Parsons chairs, a steel *château* table, Kravet's deep, curved banquette and crystal candlesticks—a mainstay of the well-dressed table—give minimalist décor maximum impact in a condominium with an open floor plan. Further amping up this dining area's appeal is a chic chandelier from Hector Finch, London, available through Zoffany. Fabric is Chivasso, a division of JAB. Uber-chic mixed media paintings on panels with high-gloss resin finish are by Marissa Starr.

rise to the perennially popular Louis XV *bergère*, an upholstered armchair with closed sides out-lined in an exposed, carved-wood frame. Reading stands, small writing desks and tables with flowing lines also became talking points.

A more formal aesthetic once again followed the excavation of Pompeii (1748), sparking fervor throughout Europe for antiquities that offered a glimpse of former royal splendor. Neoclassicism came to define Louis XVI style with legs on tables and chairs carved to resemble fluted classical columns. Gifted cabinetmakers enticed to France from Italy and Germany hastened the decline of gilding by favoring mahogany imported from the New World, which most elected not to embellish. (In contrast, attention-grabbing ebony was the timber of choice of seventeenth-cen-tury *ébenistes magnifiques*—a distinction with more than a dash of exclusivity conferred on skilled artisans.)

At the same time, the people of Provence lived simply, often lodging under the same roof as their animals while drawing their livelihoods from the land. Today this region is awash in new villas with terra-cotta tile roofs. And restored farmhouses stand amid the tumbledown barns gracing the sun-blessed countryside as outsiders lured by the area's intrinsic charm invest locally. Yet, even as symbols of rural France fade, villagers remain true to their roots. Clinging to their quiet way of life, they savor the simple pleasures of growing vegetables and herbs, dining *en famille* and layering settings with comfort and ease, collectively sending an unassuming mes-sage—a value deemed just as important nowadays as in their great-grandparents' era, when the same linen was used for fabricating curtains as for making grain and flour sacks.

But then, for some time now, gentrification has been freeing *classique* French furniture from its historically formal association, mostly in revived neighborhoods of the capital closest to the center of the city. (Perhaps nowhere more so than the trendy 11th *arrondissement*—the most densely populated district in Paris—stretching west to the fashionable Marais in the 3rd *arrondissement* on the Right Bank of the River Seine.) No longer content to live in the suburbs and commute to Paris—the seat of much of France's cultural, financial and political power—waves of young professionals are migrating to the capital, where they can walk to work or rely on public transportation, sans the need to invest in a car. As a result, living spaces have become increasingly approachable.

To this day, the eighteenth century is thought to have been the most elegant era in European history, with French furniture from this period justly singled out for praise. Symbolizing good taste and wealth: a Louis XVI *bergère* (upholstered armchair with enclosed sides and exposed wood frame)—worthy of Marie Antoinette herself.

Within the walls of regal-looking Haussmann-designed stone façades are immediately recognizable signatures of national identity that elicit admiration: finely crafted wood pieces in various finishes, splendid mirrors and *grand-mère's* lovingly cared for linens. But in this age of merging sensibilities, European midcentury modern furnishings—both vintage and new—also prop settings.

Amidst abstract works of art hovering on walls, hand-rubbed painted furniture pieces mingle easily with budget-friendly finds from assorted cultures, such as wool rugs and hand-embroidered linens from India, and pottery, artisan-made pillows, throws and vintage textiles from remote markets in Morocco, which was once a French protectorate (1912–56).

Disarmingly affordable furnishings—if not reflecting one's travels, then clearly suggesting varied interests—inevitably instill an aura of unassuming luxury in signature Gallic décor. And yet, as if by agreement, seldom do habitués stray from their unified approach to decorating, no matter in which of metropolitan France's twenty-two administrative regions one happens to reside. Whether furnishing a *château* in the Loire Valley, *bastide* in Provence, manor house in Normandy or the ultimate retreat—a *pied-à-terre* in Paris—an enviable mix of passion and panache, style and resourcefulness sits behind most every imposing door. Aesthetic visions vary, of course, but when it comes to expressing beauty and taste, countless fundamentals are firmly fixed in French minds.

Perhaps much as Louis XIV intended, the Gallic *art de vivre* has long intrigued and influenced millions while steadily swaying markets around the globe, with significant help from social media in the past decade. Little wonder, then, that we would want to take a close look at the French ever-so-chic way with design, draw inspiration from canvases ranging from cosmopolitan to provincial, and ultimately let our creativity take flight.

—BETTY LOU PHILLIPS, ASID

Sanders Studio, Dallas, striped, primed, painted and glazed—with old-world know-how—once nondescript chests, giving the pair a dramatic, more modern identity. Hollow, handblown Venetian glass lamps from Donghia rest on inset antique mirrored tops, another posh update to night tables whose height now matches the mattress's pillow top. Empress Eugénie, wife of Napoléon III, prompted the fashion for lace-edged bed linens. The town of Calais, on the shores of the North Sea, is the lace capital of France, though Chantilly and Valenciennes are also famous centers.

FLUENT FRENCH

ARMED WITH EDUCATED EYES, unerring taste and amazing confidence, is it any wonder that the French have long held the design world in its thrall? Or that the majority buy what they like, boldly upholding the standards they insist upon while instinctively styling settings that do not appear "decorated," but rather reveal their passions, interests, heritage and unmistakable flair—to say nothing about how they want to be perceived.

To put it politely, many raise their well-groomed eyebrows at our dependence on decorators, whom they view as leaving one vulnerable to uncertain, *not* necessarily enviable, results. Specifically, it is not that none would ever dream of collaborating with a design professional, only that turning over control of a project even to the most capable hands is to them a somewhat unsettling thought.

So, what if faced with myriad issues that warrant assistance? In that case, the French are likely to have a comprehensive plan, opt to be hands-on and be precise in requests: specifying styles, shapes and proportions in such detail as to leave little doubt about their wishes suggests the confidence they have in their own good taste, which is, of course, an extension of their identity. Never mind that ancestral furniture and *objets d'art* delivered with alluring backstories

In keeping with the current rage for Belgian linen, the designer's South of France atelier produced curtains with sensuous folds, while artisans at Flamant, Paris, crafted and then covered in linen the Louis XVI chair. Flooring is centuries-old *parefeuille,* original to the *bastide.* Salvaged terra-cotta, highly coveted for restorations both in France and abroad, is available in the U.S. and Canada through Ann Sachs Tile and Stone.

Not far from the ancient village of Oppède-le-Vieux—a small town that served as an administrative center for the papal state of Avignon in the Middle Ages—a nineteenth-century *bastide* in serious disrepair languished vacant. Swayed by the property's potential, a Canadian family proceeded to restore the façade and give interior spaces more than a little polishing. The result: the ultimate summer house with a private vineyard and twenty-first-century amenities. (Villagers in the South of France deem a two-story *bastide* more chic than the humble one-story *mas*.)

conspire to make seeking expert help unnecessary. The French are the first to admit it.

Without fail, settings start with furnishings handed down from one generation to the next, reflecting disparate influences and periods; this is to say, a blur of Louis styles that eases formality. As rooms take shape, they gather even more history-laden accoutrements that meaningfully transform the space. Suffice it to say, in France, collecting is a national pastime; some would call this propensity for hunting and gathering a personal mania. By all appearances, habitués spend a lifetime closely guarding their artistic heritage both for themselves and for their children. For some, the thrill of the hunt is addictive. Yet even the most zealous contend that less is more, for there is fear of cultural backlash against ostentation. Displaying riches like museum artifacts is frowned up, which is to say *déclassé*.

Despite the grandeur in which Louis XIV and his descendants, Louis XV and Louis XVI, lived in the sumptuous Château de Versailles, understated beauty is a design dictum. Those with pro-Gallic sentiments equate elegance with restraint, shunning the wanton excess identified with the *ancien régime* ousted in a bloody revolution that began on July 14, 1789, when thousands of proletariats stormed the Bastille, freeing prisoners and ushering in a decade-long Reign of Terror starring a guillotine stationed in the center of Paris.

Impressive setting? To be sure. Three mountain ranges in the middle of Provence frame the Luberon region, with towns and villages nestling north and south.

Not that there aren't glints of glamour inside *appartements* in the Île-de-France—the very heart of France, including Paris and seven surrounding *departments*—where more than twelve million people live. (By some estimates, fewer than 25 percent live in single-family homes.) In *boiserie*-bedecked quarters that all but demand splendor, the extravagance—layers of marquetry and ormolu, not to mention brocade draperies with heavy swags and jabots—would have surely delighted the Bourbon monarchs. Most settings, though, are neither fussy nor stuffy. With the cardinal rule of Gallic upbringing being that wealth and discretion must go hand in hand, care is taken not to flaunt indulgences that are showy trappings of success, much less break the age-old cultural taboo of appearing as though living stylishly is a preoccupation in itself.

Tellingly, of course, eighteenth-century furniture with carved ornamentation springing from one of continental France's well-defined regions, posh textiles, distinctive porcelains and oil paintings in original carved-wood frames are instantly identifiable indicators of style and station. Much like the fine linens and heirloom silver passed down from one generation to the next, all are celebrated badges of the fortunate, having bearing on how one is perceived. But, then, so are less-than-perfect antiques that look as if they have overstayed their welcome. An area rug that is threadbare in places, a chair with fraying fabric, porcelain with chips and cracks all telegraph privilege, if not serve as a reminder that perhaps those of us living an ocean away shouldn't try quite so hard. No matter that in our image-obsessed society it is a challenge to avoid taking decorating too seriously.

Wary as the French are of outward ripples from peers, there is, however, the unmistakable sense that their more-than-mild obsession with appearances remains intact. Marrying luxury with utility in refreshing, at times unexpected ways at once inspiring and intriguing results in settings both distinctive and yet familiar with a hint of *je ne sais quoi* that is difficult to explain.

Whatever one's sensibility—modern or classic-minded, or a blend of tradition and modernity that in recent years has taken hold—it makes little difference. The warmest, most approachable settings begin with space management that not only increases the visual appeal of a room but also enhances its livability.

Put simply, traditional interiors favor symmetry, or mirror imagery, historically the key to classical style. But even when identical furnishings sit facing each other on either side of a fireplace or other vertical axis, a subtle bit of asymmetry may fittingly find its way into the room. Atop the mantle, for example, a grouping of mismatched candlesticks parked to the left may offset a small sculpture set to the right.

Asymmetry paves the way for appealing modernity, pulling from unrelated, age-appropriate pieces that work together in an inviting way. Options abound for deftly shaping a conversation grouping: from disparate chairs separated by a small table sitting across from a sofa, rather than another sofa, to perhaps four chairs diagonally situated across from one another forming the letter X, with a round coffee table at the center.

Having a strategy has obvious benefits. Here, then, are more basics worthy of note, which is not to suggest that they are unique to the French, only that Gallic instincts together with significant planning have the capability of enhancing the allure of any room:

◆ FURNITURE ARTFULLY SET ON AN ANGLE OPENS UP A ROOM. Placing pieces on a diagonal, or simply angling an armoire, for example, in a corner rather than pushing it against a wall reflects the influence of the French, who have a talent for thinking inventively when it comes to crafting areas stylish and smart.

The French consider both wine and cheese part of their national identity—and pairing the two requires knowledge of both. What's more, when it comes to one of France's 400 different cheeses, the republic has its own culture. The classic school of etiquette suggests that when taking a serving of cheese, it is important to preserve the shape, as the flavor varies from the rind to the heart. (So, never cut the point off a wedge; it is a transgression to do so.) Smitten by French wines, Thomas Jefferson encouraged grape growing near Monticello, which, of course, also had its challenges.

◆ IN A SIMILAR VEIN, seating that floats in space rather than hugs the perimeter makes conversing less challenging, especially in a room with ample square footage. Before doing as the French do, however, confirm that the backs of furnishings are "see-worthy," not made of a lesser-grade material, as the flip side of some furniture pieces are. And, yes, take care that a roomy room doesn't end up seating a fraction of the number of people possible, marring the effect of fashioning conversation-friendly clusters.

◆ FURNISHINGS NEED SPACE TO BREATHE. Sturdy silhouettes require ample air space to have a positive influence on a room's character, whether a room is enviably sized or not.

◆ TWO WOOD PIECES SITTING SIDE-BY-SIDE ARE LESS THAN NEIGHBORLY. Separating hard surfaces with fabric-covered upholstery allows them to keep a discreet distance, thus avoiding the perception that something is amiss.

◆ THE TALLER THE CEILING, the more imposing the furnishings can be. However, unless a piece with a towering demeanor, such as the ever-present armoire, *bibliothèque* (literally, library), *buffet deux corps* (literally, buffet two bodies) or other iconic national symbol finds its way to the right place, its considerable presence can be off-putting, slanting the visual weight to one side of the room. Clearly, integrating boldly scaled, dignified, old wood pieces can be *très difficile*, even for the scale-savvy French.

◆ STRIKING A PROPER BALANCE, meaning artfully distributing weight, is the secret behind a room with the feeling of well-being. (As a result, it helps to place the largest piece of furniture first.) Although there need not be something in every corner

In France, the entrance hall is not merely a spot for welcoming family and friends, anymore than it is a thoroughfare for approaching rooms designed for living. Gallic standards call for gracefully rendered architectural details—as the space has the power to wordlessly set the ambiance of a house and serve as an important introduction to the interior. Certainly, it must also make a positive first impression.

basking in an imperial mirror's reflected glow, it is not by accident that in France ancestral portraits pose arrogantly on easels, taut tapestries look down from walls and folding screens brushed with painted scenes help project an air of authority, say, across the room from statuary. Or that oils, gouaches and prints swell into collections, stretching toward the horizon. Though none may tote equalizing weight, each helps view attention-grabbing furnishings in a more flattering light. Either scale (size) or proportion (shape) can result in a setting looking "off"—or in other words, with an image problem that is hard to pinpoint.

✦ FURNISHINGS, REGARDLESS OF HOW ATTRACTIVE, look best when varied in height, in the same way that layering large, lush blooms makes a flower arrangement most interesting. An ottoman may unexpectedly disrupt a stream of furnishings of equal stature while doubling as extra seating or as a coffee table.

Or any generously sized painting perched on an easel can offset a tall wood piece across the room while adding importance to a corner. A lamp, though, is the most common vehicle to an undulating setting, and its finish, or texture, will contrast with the wood piece on which it is propped. If space permits and floor outlets are available to hide unsightly cords, not to mention ward off potential accidents, a console may float behind a sofa, letting a pair of lamps create the wave of heights. Beyond that, the French take care that all lamps finish at the same height, generally ranging from 27 to 30 inches, varying no more than two inches, since eye-level lighting is most flattering.

✦ AS IT HAPPENS, generously proportioned furnishings not only attract more than their fair share of attention but also project a weightier appearance than those more refined. As a result, in tight quarters, most use high-profile pieces sparingly.

✦ YET EVEN CLOSE QUARTERS BENEFIT FROM THINKING BIG. Furniture pieces of epic proportions keep a room from feeling cluttered, while filling a room with countless small-scale furnishings will make the space look even smaller. (It is wise, of course, to confirm that the piece being considered can negotiate any turns in the hallway as well as inch through the doorway, before scaling up and paring down.)

✦ A SOFA FLANKED BY TWO UNRELATED PIECES SIMILAR IN HEIGHT, or nearly so, is more eye-catching than a sofa edged with matching tables. Ideally, the furnishing's surface should

Not by chance, a cabinet conceals the radiator, as stone flooring with a proud past joins textured walls to offer a warm welcome. A botanical simply leans against the wall.

be the same height, or nearly the same, as the sofa or chair arm it sides. Since the shift away from skirted tables, there has been a strong demand for vintage bar carts to lift settings from the ordinary.

◆ CLEARLY, IT IS FINE TO REPEAT A SHAPE. But nestling round forms, for example, amidst rectangular, square or oval ones is significantly more pleasing.

◆ COMMONPLACE OR NOT, there is always a table beside a chair, to place a glass of wine or small plate of cheese, and there is a table lamp or floor lamp positioned just so for ending the day with a book or the newspaper.

◆ TO MOVE ABOUT FREELY yet insure that a coffee table is within arm's reach (so no one needs to get up to set down a drink), the French not only allow sufficient knee space (approximately 15 to 18 inches) between a sofa and coffee table; they also gravitate to tables 18 inches tall, if not tea table height, or 24 inches tall. In modern settings, a cluster of small-scale square tables often works in place of a lone large one; or perhaps two square ottomans make a statement.

◆ DESIGN IS AS MUCH ABOUT what's left out of a space as what is put in it. There need not be something in every corner. With beauty in simplicity, it is important to know when to stop.

LEFT: Even what some would call "modest" cabinets have a purpose. Those on the right offer a place to hang outerwear, while those on the left discreetly hide plumbing. Oversized floor tiles make the entry appear larger by pulling the eye to each far-reaching corner. Glazing, more ambitious than straight paint, furthers interest.

OVERLEAF: Stone surrounds define the breakfast room and kitchen, and three steps up from the working kitchen, the formal dining area, where like tables flanking the opening are pushed together in the middle of the room for dining.

FACING: Anchoring a well-equipped kitchen is a duel-fueled Lacanche commercial range, forged in the Burgundy village of the same name—an area known for its fine food and wine. Giving the space a contemporary bent, the hood sprawls over the sink. Walls are Farrow & Ball No. 241, Skimming Stone. Steel doors open to lush plants in large terra-cotta pots. ABOVE: Texture warms a generous island that meets multiple demands. Most French households have ample stock of vintage linen *torchons* (tea towels) with embroidered stripes that elevate the utilitarian. Highly collectable are those with red stripes, which isn't to suggest they are for daily use. With *problématique* stains being far from charming, in French minds, less showy kitchen towels are fashionable. (The best place to look for those with red stripes: the Porte de Vanes flea market, Paris.)

OVERLEAF: At a table set for a family breakfast, the focus is the view: a private vineyard, a field of lavender and the rocky cliffs of the Luberon. With age difficult to capture using straight paint, somewhat more labor-intensive glazing enriches the character of cabinetry by Cuisines Fabre, Robion, France.

ABOVE: Though people with Gallic roots once failed to embrace new furniture, these days there are ample exceptions, including these gray-washed chairs. Adding personality: chair pads touting the country's ongoing affection for French wines. FACING: Half rounds host a vessel sink, while stone salvaged locally works with the weathered walls.

OVERLEAF: Although the French traditionally receive and entertain guests in *le salon*, overly serious rooms do not make sense in many homes. Rather, common spaces exude a casual aura suited to family life. Interweaving quiet neutrals (fabrics and furnishings) and rich textures (exposed beams, a sisal area rug, tile flooring and a stone *cheminée*—the latter two original to the house) promotes the feeling of spaciousness. Farrow & Ball No. 2009, "Clunch," on walls complements the earth tones.

FACING: Small pillows sit in front of pleasingly plump larger ones—with patterns starring and solids playing a supportive role—on a sofa upholstered in *au courant* Belgian linen. In contrast to a decade ago, color is used sparingly in many Provençal homes and often, prints are few. And though some American designers claim it is wrong to chop pillows (create a V in the middle), the French seemingly have no inhibitions about doing so. **ABOVE:** A *cristal* ball from Eichholtz Company, headquartered in the Netherlands, tops vintage notarized documents from the French firm Ateliers CSD.

ABOVE: The French have a way of putting their own refined spin on the common, the everyday, personalizing the ordinary while quite naturally catching others' interest. With trademark attention to detail, burlap conceals a nondescript container housing potted hydrangeas, ensuring nothing distracts from the beauty of blooms turned to best advantage. RIGHT: Grand or petite, *salons* boast thoughtfully curated accessories as bold (reproduction *étrusque* head from Musée du Louvre boutique) or understated (baskets that keep magazines within easy reach) as one's look demands. By French standards, the best scale for tables that back up to roomy 84- to 96-inch sofas requires leaving no more than 10 inches exposed on a side.

ABOVE: Leaving nothing to chance, oversized lanterns bridge the first and second floors, adding importance to strategically placed cutouts. **FACING:** In a nod to the property's vineyard, a modest wine cellar is sited just steps from the main living area.

RIGHT: In France, the second floor is a most private space designed for slumber with all its finery—lace-trimmed sheets, duvets and in some residences, intimate canopies. FACING: Easily maintained nickel fittings are more common than brass in both powder rooms and bathrooms in the French Republic.

OVERLEAF: With cultural backlash against ostentation, comfort is born in fine details and a serene palette. A towering beamed ceiling and wide-plank bleached oak flooring dress a master bedroom in chic simplicity.

FACING: To be sure, French country has dressed itself up since Louis XIII ascended the throne. Setting it apart now and forever is a kaleidoscope of styles reflecting various influences and periods, with furnishings most often drawn from the reign of Louis XV, without lavish ornamentation. (The Romans scented their baths and freshly washed linens with fragrant lavender.) ABOVE: In France's chicest bathrooms, color is a rarity. Gently scented chalk white towels, varying in size, jostle for space on gleaming heated rails. Nearby are *tisanes pour le bain* (herbal teas for the bath) in tiny cheesecloth sachets, and *savons pour le bain* (bath soaps), often made from formulas dating back centuries.

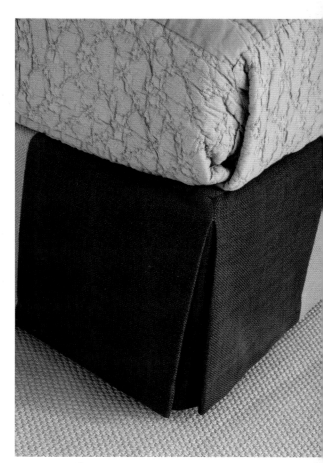

PREVIOUS OVERLEAF: Strong architectural details and soothing textures conspire to reduce the need to "decorate." Interesting but unpretentious closet doors offer clothing and bed linens breathing room.

LEFT: In Provence, there is seemingly a movement afoot as habitués spurn strong, vibrant hues, opting instead for restful neutrals. Here, myriad tones of gray and brown are bedfellows. Unrestricted by the dictates of design is a mix of textures. **ABOVE LEFT:** When it comes to design, the French obsess over details. Oversized bronze-finish nail heads and contrasting welt brings distinction to soaring headboards, upholstered in fabric by Nobilis. These days, mushroom is a popular hue. **ABOVE RIGHT:** Tailoring lends an individual, contemporary twist to an otherwise unassuming room. Coverlet is from Blanc d'Ivoire, Paris.

ABOVE: During an extensive restoration, a *bergerie* (sheepfold) was repurposed into a bedroom while retaining its shape. Also worthy of keeping and sealing from the elements was a *meurtrière* (a murder hole in a passageway). The small opening in the wall—original to the enclosure that sheltered sheep during winter months—was a source of fresh air. From it, caretakers could also send arrows sailing at predators. **RIGHT:** Not leaving clutter to chance, or for that matter clothes in need of laundering, a roomy, utilitarian basket stands ready to welcome most anything that might hamper a look.

FACING: Neutrals join forces with textures, paving the way for a bedroom to echo the beauty of the natural world. Rows of decorative trim sewn inches apart add flair to grommet window panels. ABOVE: Merging form and function brings a touch of charm to the room, while the tonal palette increases the sense of space.

No longer is exposed plumbing simply something nice to look at in upscale European hotels; it is coveted Stateside, a feature that reflects good taste. **FACING:** This being France, the bathroom boasts a wet area—with an edgy sink, a vanity ideal for storing necessities and a walk-in shower. The water closet is concealed from view behind a closed door. Among the roses, jonquils, lilacs, violets and lilies in Marie Antoinette's garden at the Petit Trianon, calla lilies grew. (Folio Corian offers a similar washbasin.)

OVERLEAF: Balancing leisure with the country's 35-hour work week is central to the French way of life. As tourists, however, surely we would miss out if we failed to visit Provence's historic sites, including the amphitheater in Arles, the Pont du Gard—a Roman aqueduct located just north of Nimes—and Carcassonne—France's most famous medieval citadel. The Romans annexed the region in about 125 BC, decades before Julius Caesar brought the rest of an area then called Gaul (now France) under his control.

DEMYSTIFYING FRENCH STYLE

DURING THE EIGHTEENTH CENTURY, France astonished the world with her masterful artisanship, setting standards of excellence that tastemakers worldwide openly admire and by which they judge Fine French Furnishings and most everything else. Along posh Paris streets lined with luxury boutiques and high-end antiques, and in secondhand shops throughout the provinces, it is both well known and accepted that the French *still* are famously hard to please, three centuries later.

Indeed, they expect a level of workmanship that, more often than not, only money can buy. Faced with the task of returning an aging manor to splendor it has not seen for years, the conventional wisdom is that some things are better left undone rather than done poorly or given a quick fix. This is why many of the more than one hundred *châteaux* built centuries ago in the Loire Valley remain in serious disrepair, leaving some with leaking mansard roofs, falling stone, rotting window frames, crumbling plaster walls, buckling wooden floors and unreliable heating, languishing unoccupied after passing from one generation to the next.

From the statement-making Bars de Montpellier reclaimed stone flooring that originally embellished a seventeenth-century *bastide* (two-story country house), to the stone surround openings (two unseen), to the eighteenth-century furnishings, there is no shortage of panache in a *hall d'entrée*. The hand-painted panels adorning the ceiling are from the same era but transported from Sicily by Chateau Domingue, Houston, the premier stateside source for European architectural antiques. Sterling roses add an unexpected note of color to the otherwise monochromatic aesthetic.

To the French, quality is paramount. Wood pieces with deep carving, tongue-and-grove joints (rooted in medieval Europe) and the patina of age are coveted. Durable, kiln-dried hardwood frames (made from oak, elm, hickory, ash or maple) and eight-way hand-tied construction are the foundations of well-crafted sofas and chairs, with legs being a continuation of the frame and joints doweled with thick wooden pins rather than simply screwed into the frame. Softwood frames (pine, cedar, Douglas fir and plywood) are less sturdy, while joints screwed and then glued tend to squeak and split over time. No matter how well made the frame or beautiful the design, comfort is key, implying an innerspring core with tempered steel springs, preferably brass-plated, and webbing secured eight ways (in all directions) to the frame.

To be sure, happiness can be prohibitively expensive. Yet to the Gallic way of thinking, settling for second best can equate to a pricey lesson when that affordable alternative begets short-lived joy. (Or, worse, needs replacing in a few years.) Therefore, offering no apologies for their relentless search for quality or appetite for elegance, furnishings are the best one can manage, testifying to one's impeccable taste.

Like most people, the French splurge on things that are important to them and economize on others. As *châteaux* increasingly shutter their doors, invariably, some find it hard to resist bargains at the capital's famed auction house, Drouot, or when combing the Marché aux Puces de Saint-Ouen, the vast weekend flea market north of Paris, if not L'Isle-sur-la-Sorgue, in Provence, which also abounds with antiques.

With glaring beauty in intricately carved commodes, as well as deftly placed *passementerie*, the French insist that there are valid reasons why some furnishings are more expensive than others. Further, they say, it is pointless to complain, since you pretty much get what you pay for.

Confirming that you pretty much get what you pay for, these three throws were sent packing when the front and back stripes didn't line up. **FACING:** Might this dwelling take inspiration from internationally famous writer and illustrator Ludwig Bemelmans, who wrote, "In an old house in Paris that was covered with vines lived twelve little girls in two straight lines . . . the smallest one was Madeline."

So, whether one is an avowed modern minimalist who prefers interiors stripped to the essentials, has global leanings and is in awe of Louis furnishings or favors a look somewhere in the middle, in French minds:

◆ THE MOST ALLURING SETTINGS EVOLVE OVER TIME; they are not thrown together overnight. It is entirely apt, then, to have rooms in varying stages of progress, hinting of possibilities rather than straining one's budget. Quickly filling empty rooms with shiny new furniture is all right for some people, but not for the French.

◆ TO THEIR WAY OF THINKING, it is inexcusable to live in a house full of meaningless pieces with no ties to the past or any sentiment attached, and even worse, one furnished at a hurried pace with pricey objects lacking character. For them, charm lies in time-honored armoires made in scattered provincial towns and other furnishings wearing original paint, preferably collected over generations. The pressure to think twice before infusing a room with furniture is a deterrent ingrained in the French national psyche.

◆ INTERIORS MERIT FURNISHINGS WITH PRESENCE. For centuries now, a propensity for heroic-sized pieces has held sway. Regardless that large houses throughout France have gradually given way to less spacious ones with smaller rooms, the need for imposing furnishings that lend distinction remains etched in minds largely unchanged. And since this is the scale the eye is accustomed to seeing, it is maneuvered into enlarging its perception of an area, until somehow even cramped quarters appear larger, while grand rooms become more palatial still.

◆ BEYOND THAT, FAMILY HEIRLOOMS ARE WORTHY OF PRIDE OF PLACE. Traditionally, the French reserve their deepest affection for tangible links to caring ancestors who lived centuries apart. For them, cherished objects, formal portraits and a blend of furniture cut from different woods in different eras and thoughtfully handed down generation after generation offer the reassuring feeling of the familiar while placing a strong claim on the heart. No matter that these legacies might appear to need some cosmetic help. Signs of time, not painstaking restorations bent on stripping away years, add to their old-world panache. And though frequently somewhat overwhelming for their less roomy new settings, most are thrust into prominent spots where they garner certain deference by virtue of age.

◆ CONSISTENT WITH DISCIPLINED GALLIC UPBRINGING, more than necessity must prompt the desire to buy. While most of us readily admit to a predilection for immediate gratification, the French are capable of living for years without a rug, tapestry, commode or other object of desire until a *pièce de résistance* comes along that is within their reach and clearly worth the wait. This means a finely crafted piece with the requisite presence and the patina of age, if not one firmly rooted in their heritage.

◆ HARMONY IS MORE IMPORTANT THAN CONFORMITY. While some in the States crave five-piece place settings of the same china, our French cousins do not. In fact, most frown on matching sets of anything. For them, a bedroom "suite" or so-called dining room "set" with wood finishes boringly alike would be too dismal to contemplate. In homes that want for nothing, disparate elements, each with its own centuries-long résumé, come together in a predictably sophisticated fashion.

◆ INTERIORS MUST REPRESENT A CULTURE THAT SHUNS HAUGHTY EXCESS. Layering the unassuming with that more grand—or if you will, integrating princely furnishings with humble finds every bit as intriguing—makes it clear that good design is not about wealth but rather personal style and taste.

◆ WHEN IT COMES TO ANTIQUE FURNISHINGS, PAIRS ARE HIGHLY PRIZED. There is some debate, however, about the number appropriate for a given setting—on this side of the Atlantic, that is. Two is safe, not counting wall sconces and chandeliers, the most opinionated stateside designers say.

The International Building Code sets stairway regulations, though local ordinances may alter these policies. Here, reclaimed limestone walls and flooring project an ease associated with life in the South of France.

FACING: Adding to the room's identity: reclaimed beams, salvaged stone countertops and a seventeenth-century stone sink used for making goat cheese in a monastery outside the once-walled city of Avignon. For much of the fourteenth century, Avignon served as the capital of the Christian world, as newly elected French Pope Clement V opted to settle in this small town in 1309, rather than in Rome. ABOVE: Myriad textures and practical, low-maintenance elements indigenous to Provence, define a stateside kitchen worthy of the French.

ABOVE: Eighteenth-century walnut brackets rescued from an unassuming *mas* (stone farmhouse) offer antique lanterns a proper parking spot in the kitchen. FACING: An enviable supply of olive oil—used in cooking, pharmaceuticals and fuel for oil lamps since 2500 BC—hails from the much lauded Château d'Estoublon, granted AOP (Protected Designation of Origin). Adding to the *château's* considerable cache, it is the setting for a popular French television series, *Les Gens de Mogador*.

OVERLEAF: In an era of private spaces, a family room slash His and Her study slash hearth room exudes more than a dash of restraint. Behind closed doors sit the works of those with literary inspirations, but it is the masterful mix of building materials and intricate craftsmanship that bestows distinction.

ABOVE: In homage to Italy, eighteenth-century Tuscan stone stair toppers line a back stairway. FACING: Minimalist room? Yes, but dramatic—as space limitations did not justify scrimping on style. Nineteenth-century amenities— stone walls, patterned flooring, door and hardware—are note-worthy backdrops for a powder room sink with a *petit* silhouette.

FACING: Drawn to the earth's resources strewn nearby, the people of Provence built modest stone dwellings and unpretentious timber-frame houses, each with its own color palette. Using centuries-old rubble stone from a *mas* in the popular Luberon region, an enclosed courtyard was constructed in the States. ABOVE LEFT: With those living on this side of the Atlantic increasingly moving outdoors, the demand for eighteenth-century fountains is well documented. ABOVE RIGHT: In early times, the French mended broken pottery with thin pieces of iron; thus these "stapled" pieces are highly sought after today.

ABOVE: The stone sink and countertop originally garnished an eighteenth-century *mas* in Dordogne—a *département* in the southwestern France region of Aquitaine, between the Loire Valley and the Pyrenees that takes its name from the Dordogne River that runs through it. The long table nearby is ideal for arranging flowers and perfect for hosting a dinner party. **FACING:** In 1684, French architect Jules Hardouin-Mansart designed an *orangerie* (a building similar to a greenhouse) to shelter Louis XIV's 3,000 potted orange trees at Versailles. Soon, fashionable European residences flaunted similar structures with thick, frost-proof walls where citrus trees in planters could winter under cover. Millenniums later, a grand but neglected glass-topped structure with a cinderblock base underwent a renovation worthy of aristocrats. Lifting off the former, stateside residents rebuilt the base and then repositioned the top.

ABOVE: Orderly gravel pathways frame geometrically organized plantings, paying tribute to widely admired André Le Nôtre, the king of formal landscape design. He succeeded his father, Pierre, as head gardener of the Jardin des Tuilleries in Paris and later created the formal gardens at Versailles for Louis XIV. RIGHT: A stone fountain that once graced the courtyard of high-ranking members of the Catholic Church in Lyon, the third largest city in France, now casts its reflection in the waters of a stateside pool.

SALON SAVOIR-FAIRE

LE SALON PAR EXCELLENCE IS, indeed, a work of art, awash in France's storied culture and splendid architecture. Often, however, it is a setting's tangible links to caring ancestors who lived centuries apart that make the most abiding impression.

Unlike family castoffs that dwell in stateside homes only until we can afford to replace them, the French savor the pleasure and prestige of furnishings that come their way, thinking of themselves as stewards of the past entrusted with pieces of history fit to reign forever in the most coveted spots.

But, then, who could begrudge an armoire—the celebrated source of Gallic pride—such regal treatment? Built in the thirteenth century for storing armor, then housing an entire family's clothes and other sparse possessions, the armoire has risen to iconic social status since becoming emblematic of French country life. (Closets were not common in dwellings until the twentieth century.) Variations abound, so comparisons are inevitable, of course. And, certainly, some do stand well above the fray. Most prized of all are those with deep carving, shaped bonnets, piercings and the patina of age—the distinctive luster resulting from centuries of exposure to heat, humidity and light, to say nothing of oil from loving hands, being that the first thing people often do is touch a piece of furniture.

Time-honored Bennison—with its textiles borrowed from eighteenth- and nineteenth-century pattern books—gracefully flanks the door. The sconce is original to the *bastide*. The painted tin coffee pot is mid-century (about 1950).

ABOVE: When it comes to integrating architecture and design, the French seemingly come by the trait naturally. The chandelier's stately scale is in keeping with the grandeur of the ceiling height. RIGHT: In a family living area where the palette doesn't stray from neutrals, frills are kept to a minimum. Against the limestone fireplace leans an antique bellows.

Yet the consensus is that looks are not everything. Whether modest or magnificent, the point of pride confirming value and status is provenance—a document authenticating origin and chronicling previous ownership, including identifying the experts who have vetted the piece in the past. Even an armoire that might not ordinarily merit a second look commands respect when accompanied by a paper trail of its meanderings. Then, too, any tale—real or far-fetched—adds immeasurably to the cachet, readily enhancing its worth.

No matter that an armoire may unavoidably overshadow other elements in the room. For centuries, the French have favored large-scale furnishings of noble proportions. And how could it be otherwise? As large *châteaux* throughout France have given rise to smaller *maisons* and less-spacious *appartements*, it stands to reason that furniture would still have the imposing look expected when the custom of handing down family heirlooms remains unchanged.

Predictably, then, the armoire isn't the only heirloom reestablishing its preeminence. Rock crystal (colorless quartz) chandeliers, *trumeaux* (painted overmantels) and screens with painted scenes help steep settings in mystique. Meanwhile, densely woven tapestries peering down from walls paint salons with further importance. Traditionally, mirrors add drama, radiate luxury and magnify square footage with ease, whether resting comfortably on fireplaces or not.

ABOVE: Chimes that once welcomed worshippers gathering for church services now announce dinner at the Bastide de Sivergues, minutes from Apt in the Luberon Mountains. FACING: An early-twentieth-century cupboard adds to the old-world panache of the nineteenth-century *bastide*. No matter that many people are moving from large *châteaux* to homes more manageable, sought-after eighteenth-century furnishings, once in ample supply, are increasingly difficult to come by.

Here are more guidelines to stylish salons with pared-down glamour in keeping with the mood of today:

◆ IN THOSE *SALONS* THAT WANT FOR NOTHING, chairs of different sizes and ages are telltale signs that settings have evolved over time. Strictly speaking, there is an unwritten rule requiring an equal number of places in the *salon* as in the dining room so guests can debate the merits of a recent film if not participate in political discussions, even after a lingering meal followed by dessert. For one to simply pick up and leave without engaging in further discussion is considered socially incorrect, as then a dinner party is thought less than successful. Obviously, to do as the French do one can always import chairs from the dining room to accommodate guests and keep the conversation flowing.

◆ IN BYGONE ERAS, IMPERIAL-LOOKING *RÉCAMIERS* (reclining chaises with one end slightly taller than the other and gracefully curved; named for Mme Récamier), settees, *bergères* (fully upholstered armchairs with enclosed sides and exposed wood frames) and *fauteuils* (upholstered armchairs with open sides) stiffly hugged the perimeter of a room. These days, artfully grouped seating—including ottomans and chaise longues parked in front of fire-places—make it easy for people with an appreciation for the decorative arts and a passion for intellectualizing to discuss most anything, including pressing concerns. Ingrained in polite society is an aversion to talking about personal finances or materialist attachments, however. And never would one ask others what they do for a living.

◆ WHILE SOME PEOPLE PREFER LETTING BARE *PARQUET DE VERSAILLES* or stone put on their own floor show, others are drawn to the beauty of hand-loomed orientals. Purists, though, favor timeworn Savonnerie area rugs, once woven for royalty, and faded Aubussons with their tapestry-like weave, as these add an air of dignity. Those rugs passed down through the ages are welcomed regardless of size. Stewards of French history disregard the stateside prac-tice of leaving eight to eighteen inches of exposed wood around the perimeter of a room. Instead, ample-size area rugs cross boundary lines, making smaller carpets appear skimpy— and rooms look larger than they are. (No matter if a rug sprawls into the traffic path.)

A kitchen dons a modern bent yet preserves its architectural strength, albeit rearranged. As if indifferent to changing times, the room remains on the ground floor, much like servants' kitchens in earlier eras that were far from dining rooms to avoid scattering fires, sounds and aromas. The countertop here is easy-to-maintain quartz, which is harder than marble, thus more durable. Cuisines Fabre in Robion, France, fabricated the cabinets.

Personifying the spirit of Provence, street markets brim with handpicked vegetables, fruits and flowers in addition to fish, meat, cheese and pasta. Electrical outlets—recessed in the quartz countertop—are ready to be of service.

✦ YET, WITH THE COUNTRY'S 8.8 MILLION DOGS CLEARLY HAVING THE RUN OF HOUSES, practicality is often a weighty consideration influencing design choices. Scores applaud durable sisal, though it doesn't react well to water. In fact, water can leave bleach-like blotches on some sisals. Humble jute, coir and sea grass—used for centuries—also epitomize today's easy ways and do not react adversely to water. Not everyone loves natural grass rugs, however. Dozens find the texture too abrasive for bare feet and infants' knees, causing it to lose some of its cachet. All steer clear of wall-to-wall carpeting.

✦ TAILORED SLIPCOVERS WITH COUTURE-INSPIRED DETAILING—piping, corner pleats and flat rather than frilly skirts—aim to protect seating, with luxurious fabrics hidden underneath. For that matter, they also camouflage weary furniture, giving pieces a fresh look far less expensively than replacing or reupholstering tattered textiles. At their intimate best, they add polish to looks by fitting sofas, chairs and ottomans *perfectly*.

✦ WITH STRONG, STATELY ARCHITECTURE—the foundation and framework of French pride— graciously scaled *salons* echo with cherished, avidly collected antiques, faithfully honoring

Let there be statement-making lighting over the kitchen island. Wave lights from the Italian company ELICA house an extractor fan, while a flock of brightly colored, hand-painted chickens perch above appliances, adding a little fun, to say nothing of a decorative accent. On a rooftop terrace at Versailles, Louis XV installed an aviary so he and Madame de Pompadour could indulge their passion for raising chickens and other birds.

the Republic of France. Even in close quarters, the French think big, opting for a few furnishings, always exaggerated in size rather than modestly scaled.

◆ STILL, UNASSUMING ELEGANCE MUST MINGLE WITH EASE. So even tightly edited spaces host heroic-sized family portraits, photographs in frames, pillows, throws, candles and freshly cut flowers arranged *en masse*. Heaped high on coffee tables roomy enough to hold chessboards are well-read books. Often noticeably absent, however, are plants, as many feel they should be relegated to outdoors.

◆ STURDY BUT SHAPELY SIDE TABLES THAT WITHSTAND THE RIGORS OF PLAYFUL, ever-present dogs offer places for glasses of France's prestigious wines and plates of the country's endless varieties of cheese. Always there are plump pillows stitched from vintage textiles to rest against and supple throws that look equally pretty front and back draped romantically, not by chance.

With centuries of expertise, France continues to be the world's leading producer of fine wines. While most on this side of the Atlantic follow the old rule "red wine with meat and white wine with poultry and fish," the French drink red wine with all but seafood. What's more, they attribute both their life expectancy of 82 and low rate of coronary heart disease to quaffing down wine with meals.

FACING: Botanicals add to the charm of a guest room with headboards upholstered in Bennison Fabrics. Bed skirts wear a modest ticking stripe. Once, tightly woven ticking was the traditional covering for French mattresses stuffed with cotton and horsehair; the stripes hid imperfections in the weave. Nowadays, however, the fabric is no longer bedridden. Rather, it traverses everything from upholstery to lamp shades. LEFT: Light pours from the entry into the upper hall, where an eighteenth-century *trumeau* (painted overmantel)—a mainstay in many French homes— hovers over a tufted bench covered in biscuit linen.

LEFT: In Provence, antique embroidered quilts pass from one generation to the next. And in families not blessed with inherited ones, new *boutis* with heirloom potential are wished-for gifts. The art involves hand sewing together two large pieces of cloth and then filling the coverlet with batting, rather than piecing together disparate fabrics to transform the quilt into the sculptural form with which we are familiar. **ABOVE:** Blue crystals echo a hue in the room, making the fixture a perfect complement. The late-nineteenth-century chandelier is from the Paris flea market.

ABOVE LEFT: Louis XVI was the first French king to enjoy a bathroom with a deep soaking tub—as not until the mid-eighteenth century did rooms at Versailles accommodate bathtubs. Tile takes its color cue from the toile. Toile-de-Jouys originated in the town of Jouy-en-Josas, near Versailles, 250 years ago. Generally, monotone, most were printed in red, blue, green or black on white or off-white ground. **ABOVE RIGHT:** Water closets in French hotels often evoke the past. **FACING:** Bathrooms in France are rich in ideas, as elevating the common is a trait at which the French not only delight but also excel. For them, luxury is lavender soap and thick, freshly scented *nib d'abeille* towels, coveted for their exfoliating properties. In the States, we refer to the same towels as "honeycomb."

LEFT: Moody gray walls, a stone-colored headboard covered in Belgian linen and white matelassé bedding join forces to bring a modicum of romance to a guest room. *Matelassé,* French for "padded," is woven on a jacquard loom, producing an embossed, quilted look. **ABOVE:** Light streams into a guest suite with an iron bed and the soft colors favored by Madame de Pompadour.

WHAT'S
AU COURANT?

WHILE THE COLOR WHEEL is a universal tool considered helpful in pairing hues, the French brush off any suggestion that world authorities can improve on nature, whose endless color possibilities coexist in harmony. As proof, they offer a blur of visual interest and drama, often straying beyond conventional combinations to more distinctive, unexpected choices after focusing on the use of the room and changing light, both natural and artificial.

No matter that more than a century ago French chemist Michel Eugène Chevreul's pioneering work as director of Gobelin, the famous tapestry and carpeting manufacturer, contributed to the development of the color wheel. Given that the Republic's climate and terrain vary from region to region, most people prefer trusting their instincts—reflecting the diversity of the natural world or the stately façades of historic sites. From the warm waters of the Mediterranean Sea to the lush, lavender-filled hills of Provence to the imposing architecture of Paris' 6th *arrondissement*—the City of Light's literary heart—the visual landscape of France influences Gallic color palettes.

Mixing subtle values of the same color family appeals to the uptown sensibilities of Parisians, whose cosmopolitan style requires that wall

While the typical French *jardin potager* (kitchen garden) germinates outside, it need not. Here, herbs prop on a windowsill, where abundant light insures that a ready supply of dill, basil, chives and more will soon be within easy reach. The polished nickel faucet with integrated spray is by Kohler; stainless steel sink is Franke, 16 gauge. The lower the gauge, the thicker the grade stainless steel, which means fewer dents are apt to occur. Roman shade sports Quadrille fabric and Samuel & Sons trimming.

finishes, fabrics and furnishings simply complement each other rather than compete for attention.

Vibrant colors appear garish in the capital's soft light, while luminous, subdued shades such as oatmeal, crème fraîche, parchment, putty and greige (a mix of gray and beige) project sophisticated airs that capture the unmistakably chic mood of the city. In pursuit of beauty, some scrape centuries of paint off walls, trying to unearth the original color or at least one suggestive of what once was. More, though, see no need to make any changes to a place filled with memories, since dwellings often remain in the same family for generations.

Contrary to common belief, those living in Provence also shy away from intense, saturated hues—although outsiders continue to associate Provence with the brilliantly colored Provençal florals and paisleys that have draped outdoor markets in a charming way ever since Avignon became home to Souleiado textiles. It isn't that these prints are off-limits. Only that for a while now, habitués have been gravitating to palettes

Nudging a kitchen beyond the ordinary are Baroncelli hand-blown Murano glass pendants that drift over an island decked in quartzite—the stone that is having its moment. Stainless steel Sub-Zero refrigerator sides a Wolf range, which is recognizable with or without red knobs. Outdoor-friendly enamelware—classic white with blue rim and vintage charm—parks in restoration glass-front upper cabinets until called into use for relaxed entertaining. Hand-brushed glazed cabinets infuse the room with innumerable shades of gray. The base? Farrow & Ball No. 229, "Elephant's Breath."

FACING: Just because pantries are common stock doesn't mean one needs to look predictable. Here, organization is a staple. **ABOVE LEFT:** Traditionalists might favor the look of woven baskets (see page 33), while those seeking a more contemporary spin might prefer custom-sized, steel wire baskets from Global Industrial, Port Washington, New York. With napkins today seemingly shrinking to a fraction of their former size, a group of oversized luncheon napkins— constructed from disparate Quadrille fabrics—sets itself apart from its peers. Servants at Versailles folded *serviettes* (napkins) into exquisite forms: boats, swans, flowers. Runner is from Dash & Albert. **ABOVE LEFT:** While using processed food is commonplace in restaurants worldwide, the renowned capital of gastronomy considers doing so an affront to the French culture. Notably, a consumer protection law passed in 2014 requires restaurants throughout the Republic to highlight those dishes made using fresh ingredients with the logo *"fait maison,"* or "homemade." A dish not labeled presumably includes some frozen food.

both muted and restrained. Earthy, subtle tones of sand, clay, biscuit, fawn, café au lait and mushroom—which appear bleached by the sun in the region's strong light—are in vogue.

For a romantic air, the look may refreshingly include a pastel. But rather than pair it with other pastels, locals prefer mixing one with airy whites, ivories, parchment and all manner of pale grays and putties, which can prove a palliative foil to stronger, more distinctive colors.

Bright, colorful accents are at home on the French Rivera in the beach cities of Nice and Cannes, where many longtime residents use a punch of color to enrich interiors, whether it is a splash of balmy yellow, poppy red or deeper claret that shores up sites flooded with light. Blue, once believed to keep all manner of misfortune away, lands in a wave of favorite shades, from the sapphire blue that bathes the sweeping coastline to the picture perfect blue in the cloudless sky. Nevertheless, the French *star du moment* is *l'indigo*—midnight blue, a black blue.

This is not to say that color doesn't make its way from faithfully tended vineyards, olive groves and wheat fields, as well as orchards with the latest crop of oranges, peaches and plums. It does. And, as if that weren't enough, the shifting shades of leafy green offer never-ending design inspiration.

Oenophiles say it is important to stock an assortment of glasses to capture a variety of wines' subtle aromas and range of flavors. Stemware for reds should be larger and bolder than for whites, colorless to see the clarity of the wine and comfortable to hold—with the vessel's foot as wide as the widest part of the bowl, for stability. Since losing our appetite for common glass, with its green edge, stemware from Ralph Lauren Home parks on lead-free Starphire shelves. Mirror backing doubles the look. Adding interest to the sidewall is a three-dimensional *papier-mâché* sculpture, *Crabe Royal du Kamtchatka*, by French artist Philippe Balayn.

FACING: Napoléon's forces, came, saw and conquered the Venetian Republic in 1797, taking away some of the city's most important artwork. *Oil of the Grand Canal*, by noted painter Mathew Alexander, a member of the Royal Society of British Artists, merits a spot on open shelves in a hall among vintage French pots, glazed blue. Barometers, dating from 1890 to 1920, that once resided in homes abroad join lanterns, creating an attractive seascape. All are from The Barometer Shop in Cushing, Maine. ABOVE: Anya Larkin "Silver Night" wallpaper is the discreet backdrop for a powder room with Waterworks fittings, Labrazel accessories and New Ravenna's "Raj" mosaic flooring laid in a chevron pattern. Dallasite Joan Cecil embroidered "Rooftops on Fourth" on linen hand towels by Sferra. Although the centuries-old desire for fine linens has not changed, people have. Responding to the challenge, Sharyn Blond Linens, Fairway, Kansas, introduced sea-related guest towels, hand-embroidered in Madeira, Spain. RIGHT: A chandelier from Chameleon Lighting projects a modern silhouette while shedding light on chevron-patterned flooring. To determine the appropriate size chandelier, add the length and width of the room, then convert the number of feet to inches for the fixture's diameter. And know that a chandelier can always profit from a professional cleaning.

Lobster Salad

1 large Orange • 2 cooked Lobster tails
shelled & chopped into bite size pieces • ½ ripe
Avocado, Pitted, peeled & diced • 1 Mango,
Pitted, Peeled & diced • 2 Scallions, finely chopped
white parts only • 2 cups mixed baby greens

• DRESSING •

2 tbsp. extra virgin Olive oil, 1 lg. lime juice, Salt & pepper

Stilton Salad

12 oz. Spring mix salad greens • 2 whole apples
cored & sliced thin • ½ Cup pecan halves •
dried cherries. • 6 oz. Crumbled blue cheese

1 tbsp. Dijon mustard • 1 tbsp. Maple syrup

1 tsp. Apple cider vinegar • ¼ cup Olive oil

Salt & pepper to taste

Caesar Salad

4 Clove fresh Garlic, Peeled, thin minced

1 Baguette, sliced thin (preferably day old) • ⅓ cup

fresh Lemon juice • 4 oz. Parmesan cheese

grated • 2 eggs. Freshly grated

PREVIOUS OVERLEAF: Enviable weather on Florida's Gulf Coast prompts leisurely breakfasts, if not alfresco luncheons on the veranda of a beach house. Place mats are by Deborah Rhodes; blue bowls from Barneys New York.

FACING: With a list of ingredients hand painted on chair backs and assembly instructions on seat cushions, a salad—the ideal light lunch—can become a reality following a quick trip to the grocery or farmers market. In England, only seven dairies are certified to produce Stilton, the king of cheeses. **ABOVE:** When Louis XIV's taste for luxury put a drain on France's assets, the king decreed that the public send all silver and gold to the treasury to be melted to pay war debts. Replacing plates with ceramic pieces boosted interest in the country's humble *faïence* (tin-glazed earthenware) industry, where layering and design go hand in hand. Bespoke dinnerware—each plate unique—by Parisian artist Marie Thurman is from Bergdorf Goodman, NYC. Flatware made in Portugal, available through Dahlgren Duck, Dallas. **BELOW:** The French bulldog, with its sweet personality, is *the* dog of the moment in France, surpassing the Jack Russell in popularity. Dogs have long had a special place in French hearts. Being the accessory of choice, they accompany their owners to cafés, museums, movies, markets and just about everywhere else. An ocean away, we can be equally obsessive about our pets. Indeed, Jackson's comfort is always foremost in mind.

The iconic navy-and-white nautical stripe—a hose-friendly Dash & Albert area rug—defines a Murray's Iron Works grouping with sofa in a Perennials solid and chairs covered in a graphic Quadrille print, accented with contrasting welt. An assorted mix of pillows is the answer to making a deep sofa comfortable. Striped beach towels are from Ralph Lauren Home. Hand-blown hurricane lanterns happened upon in sun-drenched St. Tropez—a postage stamp of paradise—add ambience to the space.

OVERLEAF: Arresting streaks of color frame a table set for easy entertaining.

ABOVE: Where better to watch the sun set, entertain friends, read a book or take a quick nap than on a rooftop? A graphic stripe covers a Dash & Albert pouf sturdy enough to serve as seating or hold a drinks tray. Playful "Aga" from China Seas gives an edge to the canopy-shaded daybed by Dedon. BELOW: The popularity of grilling outdoors shows no signs of waning. FACING: Mixing textures—rough (woven Dedon Chaise) and smooth (Perennials fabrics on chaises), soft (towels) and hard (flooring)—creates a laid-back space where an umbrella offers protection from the sun once a thunderstorm has moved on. Brushed Egyptian cotton blue-and-white-striped beach towels are from Ralph Lauren Home; those in aqua are from Yves Delorme. Defining the seating area is Brazilian Ipea, a hardwood so incredibly strong that it is impossible for a nail to penetrate. As a result, craftsmen drilled small holes in the lumber, and then screwed the deck together.

TIME-HONORED TEXTILES

IN THE FRENCH MATERIAL WORLD, fabrics, furniture, floor coverings and *objets d'art* vie with one another for the pleasure of introducing color to a room. But it's most often compelling fabrics that set the mood, whether the starting point or not.

Old-world fabrics, such as those from the grand house of Braquenié—one of the preferred textile lines—rise to the occasion, tempering the stuffiness of oak-paneled *boiserie*, while casting *parquet de Versailles* floors and antique urns turned into lamps in a new light with help, certainly, from a gamut of stylish shades. Without fail, exquisite silks, jacquards and damasks woven in France's fabled textile mills hidden outside Lyon also win considerable applause.

Fiber—either natural or synthetic—is the origin of all fabrics. Natural fibers woven from tufts of plants or animals produce cotton, linen, wool and silk. Polyester, nylon, acrylic, rayon and acetate emerge from laboratory-made synthetic fibers. Synthetics are stronger and more resistant to fading and wrinkling than pure fibers, but they are sullied by a tendency to droop and pill—and perhaps the fact that they are lower priced.

For more than two millenniums, the Chinese zealously guarded secrets surrounding the production of silk, making smuggling

Perfectly aligned braid from the family-owned French house of Houlès elevates window treatments from modest to chic. But, then, *passementerie* (artful trimming), whether braid, tape, fringe or gimp, applied to the edge of most any textile always produces a finished look.

silkworms out of China a crime punishable by death. As if leaving nothing to chance, a law also prohibited commoners from donning the fabric, as it was strictly the province of emperors and royalty. Following Marco Polo's journey along the famed Silk Road, the trade route that stretched from China through Central Asia to the Mediterranean Sea, silk mania gripped France, with people clothing themselves, embellishing their homes and treating silk somewhat reverentially. When it comes to selecting fabrics, it might help to think French.

◆ LUXURIOUS SILK, WHOSE RADIANCE RIVALS PRECIOUS GEMSTONES, communicates a subtle elegance that complements deep moldings and elegantly carved *boiserie* glazed light gray, gray-green or gray-blue. It is more grounded than historically opulent brocade woven with metallic threads, or its equally chic cousins satin and jacquard. The latter's elaborately woven pattern is produced on a loom with the same name, invented in 1801 by French weaver Joseph Marie Jacquard.

◆ VELVET LENDS A *SOUPÇON* OF GRANDEUR TO ANY SETTING, defining what it means to be fashion-forward without being overly bold. Long associated with wealth, power and the monarchy, its sumptuous pile absorbs color, whether a solid, stripe, pattern or made of wool, silk, linen, cotton, nylon or a blend. Thanks to anti-crease technology, the newest velvets are resistant to unsightly marks and folds.

◆ LINEN SUGGESTS A RELAXED MODE WHILE PROJECTING A MORE UPSCALE IMAGE THAN COTTON, perhaps the result of its higher price point, attributed in part to its being famously long-lasting. (In 1923, when King Tutankhamen's tomb was opened, the linen curtains were intact.) But its celebrated durability aside, flax fibers lack elasticity, making the weaving of linen a difficult process. And though the fabric does wrinkle easily, few view this as a downside. (Knit backing can help stabilize or prevent a fabric from stretching if used on upholstery.) Knots and slubs are characteristic of lesser quality linen.

◆ COTTON, PLAIN OR PATTERNED, evokes a carefree manner—unless, of course, the patterned cotton is from the widely revered, storied house of Fortuny. Produced on the Giudecca Island, outside Venice, Fortuny fabrics—made from Egyptian cotton woven in Italy—emit a sophisticated, dressy look.

◆ AUTHENTICALLY FRENCH, monochromatic toiles-de-Jouy grace furniture, lamp shades and walls. Story-telling rural landscapes and mythological etched scenes—printed in sepia, red, violet, aubergine or indigo on the finest cotton ground—originated in the eighteenth-century

Oberkampf factory in the town of Jouy-en-Josas, near Versailles. Toiles came to the United States after the American Revolution and remain popular today.

In France, however, a toile might be a room's only fabric, while those living in North America are more apt to incorporate a creative mix of solids, stripes and checks, always staying within the same colorway.

◆ FOR AGES, COLOR-DRENCHED COTTON PRINTS CALLED *INDIENNES*—first produced in seventeenth-century India and then interpreted in France—looked at home in laid-back Provence. Nowadays, they're mostly relegated to casual tables. And in Parisian circles, seldom are they seen.

◆ CLEARLY, THERE ISN'T MUCH CHINTZ—a printed and glazed cotton—in Parisian flats, anymore than in the South of France. Nor are there many bold florals. Stripes, spots, plaids and checks are more apt to bring pizzazz to relaxed areas.

◆ CHENILLE, CORDUROY, TWILL, TWEED AND WOOL convey a casual feeling regardless of the colorway, as textured, nubby weaves cast shadows that mask light, veiling colors and causing fabrics to appear darker and duller than they are. Among their many virtues, however, tightly woven fabrics wear better than those loosely woven.

◆ LIGHT, SUBTLE PATTERNS APPEAR MORE CONTEMPORARY than do those with obvious contrast. But, then, bold geometrics most always have a modern spin. Whether aiming for a modern or traditional look, the French knowingly let the size of the room dictate the pattern's scale. In a spacious setting, a small-scale pattern tends to vanish if not interspersed with a large-scale motif. Intermingling sizes, with solids as a backdrop, makes a positive non-verbal statement.

◆ CONVERSELY, A STRONG, SIZABLE DESIGN can overwhelm a snug space—unless used in a small dose, such as on a throw pillow. To increase the sense of space, it makes sense, of course, to follow the lead of the French: cover a sofa in a textured solid that blends with the walls, then let pattern add interest.

◆ ON CURTAINS, SHOWY GARDEN PRINTS TEND TO DISAPPEAR, and even stripes can lose their identity if not applied horizontally. But, then, wide stripes running horizontally are clearly more contemporary than vertical ones, while bold vertical stripes lure ceilings into appearing taller than reality.

◆ FOR THOSE LESS PARTIAL TO FLOWERS, there are, of course, infinite other pattern possibilities with uplifting properties: smart stripes—a favorite of Napoléon—plaids, checks, polka dots, paisleys, geometrics and animal prints. Since the seventeenth century, a spot of leopard has been relaxing the seriousness of French rooms with an unexpected trace of playfulness.

◆ FABRICS THAT MELD rather than match give depth to a room. On the other hand, the same shade of blue applied everywhere—whether called azure, cobalt, cornflower or sapphire, for example—would be going to such extremes that a room would end up looking "forced." And, to be sure, a contrived look is definitely taboo in French circles. Unlike nature, which harmoniously mixes undertones, or distinct hints of influential bases, the French long ago learned that warring tints could uproot a successful decorating scheme. Whether in the same color family or not, some blues, for example, lean toward purple, others toward red if not green or yellow. (Looking at the fabric alongside other fabrics from the same family helps in identifying the undertone. Red, yellow and blue are the most influential bases.)

◆ ON UPHOLSTERY, RAILROADING—meaning turning a solid or non-directional fabric horizontally—avoids the need for seams. The catch is that the fabric's width—generally 48 to 54 inches—can't exceed the height of the furnishing.

◆ FABRIC-UPHOLSTERED WALLS not only create the feeling of intimacy but also enhance any room's acoustical properties. Often, backing gives the fabric added strength while batting generates a softly padded look and covers any flaws on walls. Always the pattern matches perfectly; seams are ruler-straight. Around window casings, moldings and doors, double welt meets at right angles. Fabric does not pucker, nor does any glue show, putting to rest the notion that the French are apt to purchase expensive textiles and then save by upholstering walls themselves.

◆ WHETHER USING A PATTERNED FABRIC ON UPHOLSTERY or for a coverlet, patterns match perfectly, seams are perfectly straight and the pattern is centered. Always. (For protection against spills, consider some of the many commercial products available that repel liquids once applied.)

◆ SINCE A ROOM FULL OF LEATHER, whether genuine or not, can appear heavy, the French are apt to warm the look of a leather sofa with fabric-covered upholstery. Imitation leather is less expensive, easier to work with than real leather and available in myriad colors. In short, it is a modern marvel, whereas actual hides are available mostly in the 5- to 6-foot range, which can be limiting.

PREVIOUS OVERLEAF: Watery shades of blue layered against classic gray walls, furnishings that float and art depicting the land and sea prompt a compact living area to appear visually grander. The Quadrille print on chairs reinforces the casual, coastal mood, while the Travers horizontal stripe, with seams hidden in folds, draws the eye to the view. John Derian tufted field bench for Cisco Brothers wears a Cassaro chevron stripe. The stacked crystal floor lamp and side table with French leanings—both from Baker Furniture—add a dose of minimalist glamour with help from the Murray's Iron Works mirrored coffee table. Stark Carpet's platinum sisal area rug, with blind stitching and mitered corners, anchors the room.

ABOVE: "Luxury is in each detail," proclaimed Hubert de Givenchy, French aristocrat and fashion designer. In a modern take on tradition, distinctive waterfall pleats, intricately rendered, tumble from a custom sofa by Marroquin Custom Upholstery, Dallas.

Harmonious blues appear in a spectrum of shades: from the cobalt that bathes the Mediterranean (on a box from Bergdorf Goodman), to the pale blue of the cloudless Provençal sky (on chairs covered in Quadrille), to the azure of painted shutters in southern France (on custom sofa upholstered in Clarence House linen, with Turkish corners softening the pillows). Reportedly, two-thirds of the world's linen originates in a strip of land extending from France's Normandy region to Belgium and the Netherlands.

Mixing rather than matching china patterns is no longer the exclusive domain of the French. Inspired by their obsession, our tastes are more sophisticated now. Irresistibly chic underplate is by Swarovski; platinum-rimmed dinner and salad plates are from the French house of Bernardaud. Sterling silver flatware is by Buccellati. Crystal, Ralph Lauren. The jeweled napkin rings and place cards dressing the table further illustrate that we have perfected the effect. RIGHT: Curtains flow from a ceiling-mounted, steel track system by The Bradley Collection. Exposed Brazilian mahogany flooring confirms that patience isn't the sole province of the French, anymore than discreet gray walls are limited to the City of Light.

FACING: In the era of Louis XIV, a Savonnerie carpet frequently covered a banquette. Regardless of the fabric swathing a banquette today, it is important that the seat height be the same as the chairs when pulled up to a dining table. As for Parsons chairs, a Parisian at the Parson School of Design came up with the look in the 1930s. ABOVE: Exacting? Yes. Dallas master upholsterer Jesus Marroquin offers impeccable workmanship from every angle in addition to sink-in comfort.

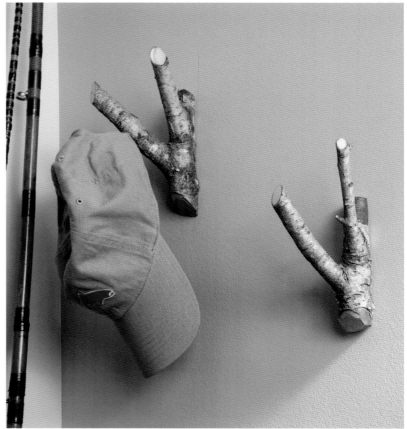

ABOVE LEFT: Bold and playful "*Les Oiseaux Blancs*," or "White Birds," a linen-and-cotton blend from the French house of Boussac, teams with grass green to keep the seriousness out of seaside living. An unbound piece of Merida sisal that morphed into a headboard introduces a bit of texture, while the artisan-made lamp adds character. Oars are old. Walls are Benjamin Moore AC 29, "San Antonio Gray," mixed with 25 percent Benjamin Moore AC 30, "Winter Gray." ABOVE RIGHT: When it comes to branch hooks for caps, jackets, whatever, it helps to have as a friend John Adams, principal of the Sierra Trim Co., Mansfield, Texas. FACING: Watercolor with a decidedly coastal vibe is by Houston artist Allan Rodewald. China Sea's "Rio" lines the back of the coverlet, with a filler adding loft. Oversized wooden buttons are from M&J Trimming, New York.

Stone pulls add an element of fun to clean-lined weathered cabinets by Baker Custom Cabinets, Naples, Florida. Phillip Jeffries burlap wallpaper and a stone slab countertop are in keeping with the spirit of the adjoining bedroom. Jars are from Michaels. **FACING:** Self-lined Calvin "Twine" stationary panels flow from a jute-wrapped rod (behind which an operable Hartmann shade filters the light), picking up on the maritime character of the weathered étagère on casters, by Thomas Love, Dallas. Open shelves offer ample space for fishing memorabilia and more. Grass green shag rug is from Stark Carpet.

WINDOW DRESSING

CENTRAL TO THE SETTINGS that harbor them, billowing window treatments screen unappealing views, guard privacy, filter direct sunlight, and, not least, solicit admiring glances. With or without dangling *passementerie* cascading down leading edges, the most enviable ones hang glamorously streamlined for a new era.

Until not so long ago, most every Parisian apartment with *parquet de Versailles* floors and *portes fenêtres* (floor-to-ceiling windows) that resemble doors resounded with grandiose curtains that not only were a definitive mark of status but did more for the fabled textile mills hidden outside Lyon than imaged. No more.

Better suiting the times, settings appear less opulent lately, certainly not as fussy. Conspicuously missing are elaborate over-the-top cornices hovering above windows, swags (yards of fabric spilling in front of the glass), and jabots (side pieces framing the pane), which many people nowadays consider a bit much if not the height of pretension. Even valences—certainly a staple in English country houses—are passé. Like cornices, they have a way of visually lowering the ceiling, not to mention making windows appear shorter than they are.

Striking, labor intensive horizontal pleats—incorporating bolts of Great Plains "Luxe Silk"—heighten the appeal of the window treatments fashioned by Straight Stitch, Dallas. In France, *chocolat* is the era's forever correct, ever-meaningful hostess gift. (Flowers—demanding attention—are not.) Quilted Bergamo "Lavello" covers the Donghia low-to-the-ground slipper chair—originally intended as a place for well-to-do women to put on their stockings and slippers, unhampered by the Victorian era's structured underpinnings. *Peonies*, oil on linen, is by American artist Sarah K. Lamb.

No question: peonies with ruffled frames stand out from the crowd, whether in the garden, at a flower stand, or a warming setting with a burst of color.

Replacing exaggerated looks that were once the norm, fabrics plunge from ceiling to floor, exalting simplicity. Yes, some curtains framing towering doors and windows tumble with style from eye-catching gilded poles accompanied by carved finials worthy of the past. But still more descend from iron rods and rings. Although points of view vary on rod placement, one glance confirms that the smartest curtains fall from as close to the ceiling molding as possible, making even small rooms look somewhat grander.

Dressmaker headings run the gamut, from pencil pleats whose narrow columns generate fullness, to fancier pleats pinched at the top, to painstakingly smocked headings where stitched latticework creates a pattern. But what makes all exceptionally alluring are some essential characteristics:

✦ TO PRESERVE NATURAL LIGHT, curtains extend beyond the width of the window twelve to fifteen inches on each side, unfailingly mirroring the scale of the room rather than upsetting its proportions.

✦ FOR *TRÈS* CHIC RICHNESS, workrooms ceremoniously calculate fabric at two-and-a-half—and more often than not, three—times the distance from one end of the curtain rod to the other, including the return (the space from the face of the rod to the wall). In contrast to ready-made curtains, which often lack sufficient fullness, there's no skimping on fabric.

✦ LIGHT STREAMING IN WINDOWS silhouettes the beauty of fashion-forward lace. But when it comes to airy sheers or gauzy fabrics that the French call *voilage*—voile, organdy, muslin, batiste—quadrupling a window's width ensures privacy.

✦ *AU COURANT* STRIPES—which Napoléon touted—make their own fashion statement while luring ceilings into appearing taller than reality.

✦ WORKING TOGETHER, LINING AND HIDDEN INTERLINING BLOCK LIGHT, absorb sound, help prevent sun damage and turn a casual window treatment into couture. But an unexpected lining—such as an irresistible plaid taffeta peeking from behind a solid silk or wool—alone, can add surprising splendor.

✦ LEST ONE WONDER, weights escaping notice stitched in deep, deep hems insure that curtains drape gracefully and then turn under in soft folds.

✦ FLOOR-SWEEPING CURTAINS simply brush the floor or "break" an inch and a half and certainly no more than three inches. It seems

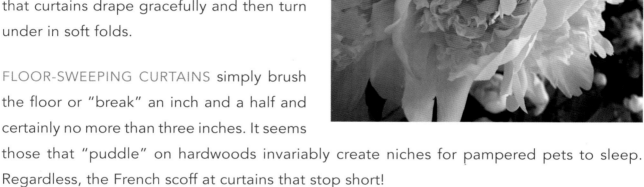

those that "puddle" on hardwoods invariably create niches for pampered pets to sleep. Regardless, the French scoff at curtains that stop short!

✦ *PASSEMENTERIE*—ROOTED IN FASHION—ROUSES INTEREST. Tassels hark back to the time of the ancient Egyptians, when they spared embarrassment by snugly keeping royal robes in place. These days, elegant tiebacks and trims have nothing to do with modesty.

✦ THOUGH NOT AS SHOWY AS THEIR FRINGE COUSINS, braids and tapes supply artful, finished borders with striking individuality.

✦ PENCIL-THIN PIPING RUNNING DOWN LEADING EDGES and streaming across the floor eliminates the need to justify the cost of tempting trim. In the words of twentieth-century tastemaker Sister Parish, "Curtains must always have an edge of an ending," trumpeting a principle of French design that American designers never tire of repeating.

✦ IN FRENCH EYES, LESS-THAN-PERFECTLY-STRAIGHT SEAMS, a pattern that fails to match, or fringe sewn in a questionable manner is any window treatment's undoing. Fabrics cascade from towering windows and descend from canopied beds with a meticulousness approaching *haute couture*, as if precisely cut and constructed by *petite mains*. But, then, the French are not apt to purchase expensive textiles and then save by fabricating curtains or bed hangings themselves, anymore than they are likely to upholster walls or undertake other tasks best executed by experts.

✦ HANDSOME, HAND-WOVEN ROMAN SHADES that softly filter sunlight without obscuring views are in keeping with today's less-is-more look or yearning for minimalism.

✦ DRESSED UP OR DRESSED DOWN, fabric Roman shades block the sun's rays and soften windows where windows would simply look like black holes at night and curtains would get in the way. Those mounted with inside brackets draw attention to impressive molding, while shades mounted outside the casing—as close to the ceiling molding as possible—make any window look larger without obstructing either the light or view.

✦ AS IF TO PUSH A SHORT WINDOW TO THE LIMIT, mounting a Roman shade under the curtains gives the window presence. Once again, the guiding rule seems to be that both should be mounted as close to the ceiling as possible.

✦ CONTRARY TO EXPECTATIONS, balloon shades have suddenly joined the ranks of over-the-top window treatments, now seldom seen anywhere.

A custom headboard, impressively hand-tufted and upholstered in understated Perennials, brings uptown glamour to a master bedroom further defined by a mix of fabrics from Great Plains. (The thickness of the padding and the density of the tufting determine the lushness of an upholstered headboard.) Taking a cue from Paris, a city lauded for its dark chocolate, walls are Benjamin Moore HC 76.

FACING: When ample drawers offer plenty of storage space—and a master bath has sought-after natural light—getting ready for the day is easy. An Osborne & Little sheer dresses the window. Sconces wear Sanderson's gray silk check, gathered on the outside, flat inside. Pale gray wallpaper with metallic flecks is by Phillip Jeffries. Waterworks' Imperial Danby, a marble quarried in Vermont, lines the roomy shower, floors and countertop, where sinks are under-mounted. **ABOVE LEFT:** Most women would find the beauty regime of Diane de Poitiers, mistress of Henri II of France, exhausting, if not extreme. She slept sitting up to prevent wrinkles, wore a black velvet mask to thwart sunburn and bathed in asses' milk, hoping to improve her skin tone if not help fill any creases. Since makeup has the power to stain a white face cloth but gray less so, the latter prop in an authentic clamshell from the South Pacific—transported to Jett Thompson Antiques, Naples, Florida, a second-home hot spot. A succulent adds a pop of color to the small clamshell. **ABOVE LEFT:** A crystal chandelier from Chameleon Lighting, London, emits warm pools of flattering light.

LEFT: With its health benefits and fuchsia undertones fading to lilac, lavender and pink, *au courant* kale's popularity rivals the fame of the 2014 Pantone Color of the Year: radiant orchid, a pale lilac with a strong pink base. Ruffled-edge "Cleybergh" vessel is by Sempre, headquartered in Belgium. BELOW: Vivid jewel-tone cup and saucer with scalloped trim is from Anna Weatherley and available in multiple colors. RIGHT: What might have become a bedroom morphed into a multipurpose room for Her, fulfilling the writer/designer's desire for mixing business with pleasure. On the walls: sophisticated *violette* (lavender), so now. Sofa with clean lines and contrasting piping boasts dog-friendly Perennials and pillows in irresistible, esteemed Fortuny. Meriting more than a passing glance is the Manuel Canovas window treatment flowing from Bradley Collection double hung steel rods. Metallic silver finishes and reflective surfaces—on shapely tables with antique mirrored tops and JAB's fashion-forward chair fabric—add pizzazz. Acrylic abstracts are by Atlanta artist Brittany Bass. Gray-lavender-and-white-striped carpet is custom, from Stark.

LEFT: There's a place for everything—books, paint and fabric samples, myriad chargers—and all are readily accessible thanks to the steel étagère by Brian Martin Metals, San Francisco, which also adds height. The fabric-covered inspiration board spurs creativity when looking out the window fails. A lavender somewhat lighter than spring crocuses paints the walls. ABOVE: Enamored with peonies, French artist Édouard Manet (1832–83) planted them in his Gennevilliers garden, and then in 1864–65 painted a series of canvases focusing on the blooms.

The BLP Waterworks four-legged Carrara marble-topped washstand—a space saver inspired by the author—is an alternative to a pedestal sink, which offers little counter space and no storage. Sconces from Urban Archeology, NYC, flanking the mirror, emit flattering light. (In contrast, a sconce mounted overhead casts unforgiving shadows on the face.) Bulgari travel-sized bath products welcome guests. FACING: Communicating luxury and making bathing blissful: Waterworks' polished nickel floor-mounted tub filler, freestanding Candide soaking tub, hotel rack and bath stool. Osborne & Little's lavender horizontal stripe wallpaper floats above the Carrara marble—named for the Italian mountain from which it is extracted.

TEXTURE RULES

A ROOM WITH FEW TEXTURES produces the feeling of space. But in the minds of the French, a fluid mix is far more pleasing, considering that a setting with all sleek finishes is unavoidably cold. Layering diverse surfaces soothes the way to the feeling of well-being by softening hard edges and adding warmth.

As it happens, texture has a reputation for shaping rooms much like color, whose opposites attract. Yet, integrating disparate materials can be a challenge, mostly because layering furniture, fabrics and lighting requires pulling together more than myriad variations of rough and smooth, to say nothing of light and dark, hard and soft, matte and shiny and refined and relaxed. Unless there is an arresting mix of both contrasting and complementary surfaces, the feeling is that a setting can be off-putting, even jarring.

Harmony is the ultimate goal. Whether expressing passion for furnishings from the era of the *ancien régime* or a taste for icons from a later period, such as Napoléon III and Empress Eugénie's eclectic, overstuffed Second Empire (1852–70) splendor, French artistry demands skillfully juxtaposing soft, sensuous surfaces with

Sheathed in devotion to France, an entry exudes welcoming warmth. Fabric from Lee Jofa swathes Louis XV chairs, flanking an eighteenth-century French buffet from Antica Collection. Both the mirror (from The Gray Door) and the sconces (from Kirby Antiques) are old, but the prints help give the setting a "now" air. All three dealers are in Houston.

those perceived severe—the more subtly, the better. Here's how the French do just that with self-assurance and skill:

◆ FAITHFUL TO THEIR HERITAGE, exquisitely fashioned, hand-forged railings wrap balconies and staircases, which is hardly surprising, given the French well-known gift for making magnificent objects from iron.

◆ UNASSUMING STONE FIREPLACES, with logs ablaze on chilly nights, worn wood floors sometimes laid in a herringbone pattern, and handsome, heavy doors often clad in original fittings temper any stuffiness in dressy spaces.

◆ IN ROOMS WITH TALL CEILINGS, exposed wood beams fuse the warmth and charm of rural France with the unmistakably urbane sensibilities of Paris, conveying the feeling of a country house far from the capital.

◆ GLAZING LENDS AN OLD-WORLD AURA TO TEXTURED, hand-plastered walls by reflecting light differently from paint, depending on the bases and topcoats used. It also calls attention to crown molding and skirting worthy of praise. White walls layered in translucent biscuit, for instance, give the appearance of worn parchment.

◆ VENETIAN PLASTER—FIRST USED IN ITALY DURING THE RENAISSANCE—borrows alluring tints such as dove, ivory and champagne from luminous eighteenth-century silks, bestowing a smooth, decorative finish with movement on walls inspired by the past.

◆ MARMORINO PLASTER, MEANING "LITTLE BITS OF MARBLE" in Italian, dates to Roman times. Comprised of lime and fine marble dust, it is semi-matte, low luster and popular in France, as well as throughout Europe.

◆ *TROMPE L'OEIL*—TRANSLATED, an artistic medium that "deceives the eye"—makes a flat surface appear three-dimensional without taking up any floor space. At the 1801 Paris Salon, the French, whose sophistication is an extension of their identity, regarded the art form as a negative. Today, however, an optical illusion that invites curiosity prompts interest and is apt to be considered amusing.

Using a dazzling Samuel & Sons tape in a refreshing way propels a bench with French influences—upholstered in a Duralee metallic—into the limelight. In this era of merging sensibilities, an oversized acrylic-on-acrylic by Aspen artist Christopher Martin further sets this gallery apart.

✦ MELLOW WOOD PIECES WITH WARM, varied patinas offer telltale signs that a site has evolved over time. An understated mix of historical periods also grounds a room with light-colored walls.

✦ TEXTURED ELEMENTS LOOK HEAVIER THAN THOSE THAT ARE SMOOTH. And bright hues signal more importance than neutrals, which often escape notice. For a satisfying look, the French use selectively elements that beg for attention.

✦ SMOOTH FABRIC WEAVES CATCH THE LIGHT, highlighting flat planes with a warm sheen that exudes a more refined spirit than nubby textures, which absorb the light and are casual. (For more on creating a mood with fabrics, see "Time-Honored Textiles," page 125.)

✦ REFLECTIVE SURFACES—crystal chandeliers, antique mirrors with blemished glass and French forties coffee tables among them—draw the eye by multiplying the light while creating instant glamour. After being maligned for most of the twentieth century—mostly because they harbored memories of war and the German occupation of France (1940–44)—furnishings from the 1940s now outshine many collectables. Similarly, mercury lamps and *verre églomisé* vases (painted on the reverse side of the glass) also radiate fresh modernity.

✦ SINCE DRAMATIC TEXTURES ATTRACT MORE THAN THEIR FAIR SHARE OF ATTENTION, the French use them sparingly, perhaps offering a clue as to why today more people favor wood finishes rather than unrestrained gilded opulence.

In keeping with classic French interiors, Venetian plaster walls are the backdrop for an aristocratic powder room that mixes the antique and contemporary. For all the apparent affluence at the Palace of Versailles in 1682, only Louis XIV had use of a bathroom with running water—and powder rooms were intended strictly for powdering one's wig. The Sun King had a collection of more than 1,000 wigs.

LEFT: A kitchen gathers yet more stars when garnished with wood beams, old lanterns and sleek marble countertops. Traditionally, the people of Provence used *pots de confit* for preserving duck or goose for *cassoulet,* if not to store other perishables. To keep the contents cool when buried halfway in the ground, the bottom halves remained unglazed. Today, jars with cracks and chips are highly prized. In contrast, those without signs of wear do not have the celebrated charm of antiques, according to many. Homegrown lemons fill the vintage dough bowl. ABOVE: Custom-made barstools sport a contemporary Lee Jofa stripe.

With ample space, a kitchen is divided into zones for prepping, cooking, dining and flower arranging. Countless vessels are at home under the sink. Clock is from Found, Houston. **RIGHT:** Trading the formality of roses for mellow sunflowers prompts a relaxed feeling; yet a sense of occasion remains. Zinc-topped breakfast table is from Memorial Antiques & Interiors, Houston.

PREVIOUS OVERLEAF: Warm woods, ample textures, clean lines and arresting tones of gray and yellow define a room for living where old meets new. Emperor Napoléon Bonaparte favored Naples yellow and used stripes lavishly in decorating both his state and private apartments. Reinforcing the far-from-opulent mood of today, D & D Drapery, Houston, fabricated the window treatment with a Schumacher print. Two large coffee tables pushed together make a bold, functional statement when within reach of sofas and chairs.

ABOVE: With both the living room and the breakfast room opening onto the veranda, the two joined forces to inspire a harmonious palette. FACING: An open-air dining area stands ready to welcome friends for lunch.

THE ART OF EXHIBITING ART

WITH ITS RENOWNED MUSEUMS and highly respected art galleries, Paris has long been a paradise for art lovers and accomplished artists. It wasn't until 1850, though, that the first gallery opened. No matter that nineteenth-century Paris was the world capital of art. Struggling artists faced the daunting task of finding venues where they could exhibit their work. The needs of those in the art world spurred France's art schools, better known as *académies*, to hold annual and sometimes semiannual exhibitions, or *salons*.

Among the most esteemed was the government-sponsored, eagerly anticipated Paris *salon*, where artists selected by a jury jostled for recognition on soaring walls stacked high with art. Since capturing visitors' attention virtually assured demand for an artist's work, competition was fierce for coveted eye-level spots.

Reportedly, the jury dismissed artists Pierre-Auguste Renoir, Claude Monet, Alfred Sisley, Jean Bazille, Camille Pissarro, Paul Cézanne and Edouard Manet, whose distinctive, unorthodox way of capturing light *en plein air* went against established tastes. To appease them, Napoléon III (1852–70) founded the now-famous "Salon des Refusés," (Salon of the Refused) in 1863, which encouraged the

When interest in art starts early, a home's art collection can grow by the week. While a large bench might appear visually imposing, a small one is perfect for hosting the day's debris. Jackets (unseen) hang behind closed doors on the opposite side of the mudroom.

There is no question that French kitchens can rightly boast of being incredibly efficient, with an array of breadboards, bowls, pots and pans within easy reach. Meanwhile, those living on this side of the Atlantic prefer tucking clutter out of sight. Nearly all favor fitted cabinets with pullout compartments, where there is a place for everything, including supplies for the artists in residence. **FACING**: Boldly patterned wallpaper by Thibaut puts an exhilarating spin on a laundry with Whirlpool units. French-inspired wire baskets are by Aidan Gray. The child's maternal grandmother smocked the dresses. Smocking dates back to the Middle Ages.

French and others to view the Impressionists with new understanding, thus shifting public perception, albeit reluctantly.

As it happens, to this day Europeans stack paintings and drawings high on walls and over doors in a manner called *salon style*. Meanwhile, half a world away, works of art loom in *moderne* fashion—that is, in a single row surrounded by ample space. Either way, displaying works of art is an art in itself, much harder than it looks, even for a people seemingly having a sixth sense for style.

It isn't surprising, then, that the French borrow tips from none other than their famous museums, which offer timeless lessons in placing art, anymore than that they embrace a few ideas of their own. Here are some guidelines worth considering:

◆ WHEREAS SMALL PAINTINGS scattered around a room disappear on generous walls, when grouped together and hung inches apart they make a strong statement.

◆ A MÉLANGE OF PAINTINGS, WATERCOLORS AND DRAWINGS can shape a single arrangement and look intriguing on a wall over a sofa that is covered in a solid fabric. (Patterned sofas distract from the people sitting on them, pointed out the late Albert Hadley, often called the dean of American decorating. Therefore, one cannot help but wonder if he also felt patterned sofas diverted attention from the artwork.)

◆ SOME OF THE MOST PLEASING GROUPINGS MASS SIMILAR SUBJECTS—say, landscapes, ladies, children, fruit, animals, birds, flowers, botanicals or architectural plates. This is not

to imply that in order to fuse seamlessly collections must be single-minded, only that a sole subject offers an organizing principle.

+ INTERMINGLING FRAMED DRAWINGS AND PAINTINGS IN A RECTANGLE—either horizontal or vertical—creates a sense of order. There isn't a hard-and-fast rule, but identically framed works look best hung approximately two inches apart; allow three to four inches between works in a grouping of various shapes and sizes.

+ IT HELPS TO MEASURE THE AVAILABLE WALL SPACE, and then use the floor to come up with a pleasing arrangement before hammering a single picture hook.

+ REGARDLESS OF SIZE, HANG WORKS OF ART AT EYE LEVEL, so that their center is at about 65 inches from the floor. Keep the same centerline on all walls of the room.

+ LARGE OR SMALL, a work of art that eclipses the rest—in value or in sentiment—is worthy of pride of place at the center of a grouping. The honor is a testament to its significance.

+ AN IMPORTANT WORK OF ART CAN ALSO STAND ALONE—preferably not in the middle of a long wall, however, if the artwork is small.

+ BEFORE PLACING ANY PIECE, consider that it is best to view some works of art close up while others are more readily appreciated from a distance.

+ A SCULPTURE should be visible from all sides.

+ A SMALL PAINTING hung beneath a larger one arouses interest.

+ A FRAME SHOULD NEVER OVERSHADOW THE ART. Then, again, an impressive frame can garner added respect for a less-than-important work of art by giving it a stronger presence.

+ MANY MUSEUMS INSIST ON PAIRING WORKS WITH FRAMES FROM THE SAME PERIOD, not that this is an easy thing to do. It is rare to find age-appropriate frames, mostly because not many survived the French Revolution, much less two World Wars.

"Let them eat cake." Clearly, Marie Antoinette never uttered those words. This tale first appeared in *Confessions by Jean Jacques Rousseau*, two years before Marie Antoinette arrived in France. At age fourteen, Maria Antonia was ill prepared for the strong resentment her Austrian roots stirred. In a political alliance arranged by her ambitious mother, she obediently married Louis August, the future Louis XVI in 1770. Mixed media on paper is by Roxbury, Connecticut, artist Gary Komarin.

◆ FOR PARED-DOWN SIMPLICITY, a stretched canvas can hang frameless against a backdrop of dramatic architecture.

◆ THE IDEA OF PROPPING PAINTINGS ON FIRE-PLACES reaches back to seventeenth-century England. At the time, lofty gilt mirrors hung above smoke-stained chimneypieces in France's grandiosely paneled rooms, coloring the capital's gray light. Some *boiserie* had oil paintings inset. Paintings also adorned the tall, narrow spaces between windows, as they still do. But these days, works of art often lean against the wall above fireplaces, too.

◆ DIRECT SUNLIGHT SHOULD NEVER FALL ON PRINTS, WATERCOLORS OR TEXTILES. Fading, yellowing and foxing can result from overexposure to light. Heat can crack oil paintings, so humidity is essential—ideally around 50 percent.

◆ NOT ALL WORKS OF ART NEED BE ILLUMI-NATED, AND CERTAINLY NOT IN IDENTI-CAL WAYS. Low-voltage picture lights often hang above paintings in Europe. Meanwhile, lighting has gone high-tech in museums and homes on North American shores.

In a twist on traditional French, contemporary furnishings paint an artfully fashioned sitting room with importance. Acrylic on canvas is by Pennsylvania artist Steven Alexander. While majestic eighteenth- and nineteenth-century Loire Valley *châteaux* made striking first impressions, inside, a damp cold often prevailed. As a result, the owners themselves frequently sat beside the fire in a small private room adjacent the master bedroom. Rather than calling these areas sitting rooms, they were known as *chauffe-pieds*, or foot-warmers.

FACING: Statement-making Arabel linen and a Duralee tape pair effortlessly, heightening the look of Louis XV chairs. Adding to the European air is the fluid window treatment, a Cowtan & Tout linen. It is the bedazzling John Richards chest, however, that eases formality, much like in classic Paris apartments, where the old mixes with the new. ABOVE: Louis XIV owned more than 413 beds. Surely, then, he would have appreciated bedding from Leontine Linens, New Orleans, the most Gallic of U.S. cities. Louisiana—named after the influential Sun King—became a state in 1812. From 1682–1763, the province was under French control, and once again, from 1800–03 when it became a U.S. territory as part of the Louisiana Purchase. Headboard is from Celerie Kemble.

TASTE FOR KITCHENS

WHILE WE FIND IT DIFFICULT to curb an appetite for professional-looking appliances and state-of-the-art cabinets, standard staples of high-style performance are often missing in French kitchens. Appliances sit in plain sight. There are few quartz countertops or family-friendly islands touting togetherness, let alone twenty-first-century computer centers lauded for their own prowess.

Noticeably absent, too, are paneled upper cabinet doors. Instead, open shelves brim with pitchers, pottery, glassware, platters, trays and other paraphernalia illustrating just how passionate the French are about their cuisine. Within easy reach, or *sous la main* (meaning "under the hand"), are *la batterie de cuisine*—the copper pots, pans, bowls and molds—dented from use—that cooks hold dear. For centuries now, master coppersmiths in the small Norman village of Villedieu-les-Poêles have forged gleaming cookware.

Unlike those of us who tend to tuck clutter out of sight in designated cabinets, the French prefer that cutting boards, *porte-couverts* (cutlery holders with knives that carve, chop, pare, peel and dice), richly glazed *confit* pots, small appliances and baskets for storing fresh bread vie for counter space with collections of tin molds: some for

Lanterns pieced together with vintage parts (by Area, Houston) and an antique cast-iron fireback (from Liz Spradling Antiques, Houston) add dimension while making a vivid statement. The roomy island works for before-game snacks as well as homework.

ABOVE: Fresh vegetables have the power to make just about everything taste better. RIGHT: Until the end of World War II, bread was mostly rounded—a shape called *boule*, meaning ball. Thus, the French word *boulangerie*, a place to buy *boules*. Later, bakers began creating the *baguette* (stick) and the *ficelle*, a skinny baguette extracted from the French word for "string."

baking, some for chocolate making and some to satisfy cravings for sorbet or ice cream. Windowsills meanwhile, flaunt mossy pots of sage, rosemary, chives and basil.

Hardwood floors sweep uninterrupted from dining rooms in some regions, while sleek black-and-white tile lends distinction in others. Far from an afterthought, unglazed, oversized squares or octagons of terra-cotta tile have the flavor of Provence, Burgundy and the Loire Valley, where clay is plentiful and there's ample charm.

In a country long the uncontested capital of haute cuisine, most kitchens are surprisingly small, thanks to everything from being more about cooking than socializing, to resisting change from the time when they were servants' domains, to homeowners who perhaps do not wish to invest in expanding and improving one's kitchen.

FACING: A stateside kitchen captures the quintessence of French country with salvaged cupboard doors, reclaimed stone countertops and a farmhouse sink. **ABOVE**: Berries, a rich source of antioxidants, are worth every calorie, whether offered at an irresistibly chic Parisian *pâtisserie* or right off the vine in Provence.

ABOVE: For the French, the ordinary seemingly holds no charm. For even the commonplace is arranged in noble fashion—if Marcel Proust's shell-shaped madeleine, made for dipping in tea, can be considered ordinary. But, then, in a sign of the times, a collegian can now major in culinary arts, and more specifically, culinary design. FACING: Behind doors transported from France sit an abundance of timeworn bowls commonplace in French homes.

After being salvaged from a property in Jura, a French village near the Swiss border, an eighteenth-century stone garden table made its way to Houston. The pitcher is from the Paris flea market.

A door from a property in France opens to a diverse collection of wine, readily accessible for entertaining. No matter that storing wine on the main floor of a home rather than in an isolated area underground brings its own set of cooling and humidifying challenges. An oversized wheel of Camembert is all that is missing. **FACING:** Whether the view is grand or intimate, there is pleasure in dining al fresco.

FACING: An eighteenth-century table that once filled multifunctional needs in a manor house in Normandy now serves versatile needs in a twenty-first-century stateside home, where it is in keeping with the kitchen's informal dress code. Dining rooms did not span the continent until the mid-nineteenth century.
ABOVE: In keeping with the French love of dogs, they are welcome most everywhere. In restaurants, they seem to know that they are expected to "sit" and "stay" at the table without whining, much like children in France are to do.

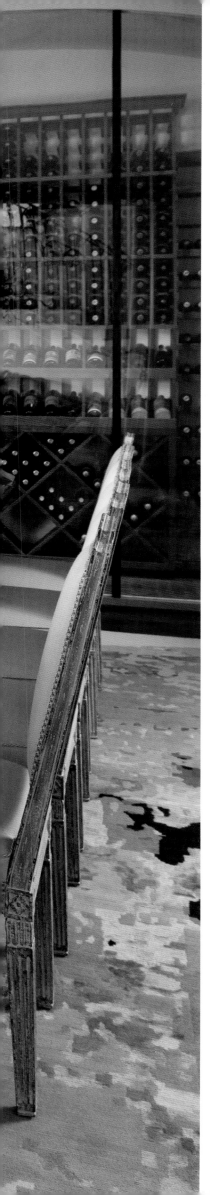

FINE DINING

BEFITTING THE COURTS of the *ancien régime*, an ardently embraced formality lingers, with proper seated dinners having all the requisite garnishes of fine dining: attractive linen cloths that sweep the floor, oversized (27 x 27-inch, or at a minimum 24 x 24-inch) linen napkins and a striking mix of heirloom china patterns, resplendent well-polished silver, sparkling crystal and candlelight.

◆ IN A COUNTRY WHERE DINING HAS BEEN ELEVATED TO ART, the handle of each piece of sterling silver flatware sits near the impeccably bedecked table's edge, while the dessert spoon and fork lie above the plate. In keeping with the French mind-set, the dessert spoon rests closest to the plate's rim, with its handle to the right, as if hinting that it may join the other spoons on the right side of the plate. Above the dessert spoon lies the dessert fork, with its handle to the left.

◆ IN CONTRAST TO OTHER CULTURES, fork tines face down, resting on the tablecloth—a custom that some say developed to undercut the fork's ability to snag ruffled lace sleeves. Others claim someone thought the tines of forks and bowls of spoons

Lustrous Venetian plaster draws the eye into a dining room—both classic and contemporary—with more than a modicum of help from the pattern-splashed Stark Carpet and the pair of eighteenth-century chandeliers from Chateau Domingue, to say nothing about the assortment of cobalt blue crystal. Buffet is from Joyce Horn Antiques, Houston. Minton Spidell host chairs wear Rogers & Goffigon velvet and Samuel & Sons trim.

looked less aggressive faced down, saying nothing about drawing attention to engraved initials without being obvious. But in fairness to the French, the flip sides liberally borrow flourishes from various chapters in French history and often are even more decorative.

✦ WATER AND WINE GOBLETS MEET DIRECTLY ABOVE EACH PLATE rather than above the knife and spoon, as in the States. A regal "underplate," called a charger on this side of the Atlantic, is integral to the table's beauty; it is removed before the first course is served, as if the aristocratic style of the French court were still central to society.

FACING: Taking to heart the French dictum that a grouping of like objects standing together has a stronger impact than if scattered around the room, a collection of geodes with striking crystal interiors rests on an Italian console among a cluster of candlesticks. Hanging overhead is a geometric form known as a "torus," a carbon fiber composite with urethane enamel, by Houston artist Edward Hendricks. (Only one of the pair is seen.) ABOVE: Flea Markets in France are the ideal place to sort through silver napkin rings, if not silver flatware, searching for initials or monograms suited to one's family members.

OVERLEAF: Living graciously calls for comfortable, generously scaled furnishings—and a setting that puts one at ease. Fabric on window treatments is from GP & J Baker. Antique console from Maison Maison, Houston; candlesticks and lantern pendants from Tara Shaw, New Orleans.

◆ CENTERPIECES ARE ALWAYS LOW—with fresh flowers straight from the garden or from local markets—so they do not interfere with conversation. (The secret behind creating stunning round bouquets is stripping away most foliage, arranging stems diagonally in a spiral, and having the outer blooms brush the vessel's rim.)

◆ CHAIRS MAY VARY IN STYLE AND EVEN BE FROM DIFFERENT ERAS; however, all are similarly scaled, meaning that, though backs may differ an inch or two, seat heights align. Typically, the French invite six, ten, fourteen or eighteen guests—not eight, twelve or sixteen—assuring that men and women alternate on either side of the hosts, who sit facing each other at the center of the table. It is a *faux pas* to separate engaged couples or those married less than a year.

◆ FURTHERMORE, IT IS NOT PROPER TO OFFER A SECOND HELPING OF SOUP or even salad and cheese or fruit, which are served after the main course. Nor is it correct to serve champagne with dessert, unless it accompanies each course of the meal. Finally, at smart dinner parties, coffee is always served in the *salon*, since most, quite naturally, have one.

◆ WHEN DINING *EN FAMILLE*, most pay equal attention to detail, taking only a slightly more relaxed approach, though by no means saving their best *faïence* for use on holidays only. The table is set with a handsome cloth that may cascade to the floor, pottery, heavy flatware and perhaps chunky bubble-filled glassware made in the village of Biot. Knife rests infuse mealtime with a sense of occasion, together with an armful of flowers that comes straight from one's painterly garden if not nearby a flower stand.

◆ AS FOR THE TABLE SETTING, it is rare to see the same pattern used throughout the meal. Whether fine china or *faïence,* mismatched services add flair. There is an expression, *bien compose*, meaning "well composed"—easily translated yet not easily explained. Like nearly all things in France, it is a question of taste. And, of course, good taste includes "plating"—the presentation, or way the food looks on the plate when served. As how it is arranged reflects the chef's artistry.

A mix of textures adds flair to even the most casual table settings.

FACING: A loggia open to the elements is more than an accessory to the house. With a fully equipped summer kitchen and an array of notable amenities, it is a getaway idyllic for entertaining *en plein air*.
ABOVE: When it is time to move the party outside, a basket of necessities can help accentuate the mood.

LEFT: For ages, dining was literally a movable feast influenced by the season—with a simple tabletop supported on trestles moved from place to place. France's first grand dining room was in the Loire Valley Château de Montgeoffroy, completed in 1776. Shortly thereafter, white linen tablecloths became commonplace in aristocratic homes. Nowadays, there is always a proper dining area, even in homes with small rooms. ABOVE: For a millennia, purple was reserved for royalty; so to this day, it has the potential of turning the most modest affair into an occasion. Fluted underplate is by Zodio, a Belgian company. The French tablecloth is from Linvosges. With purple hovering next to blue on the color wheel, and blue siding green, it is only fitting, then, that ivy clipped from the bastide's exterior walls serves as napkin rings. No matter that Van Gogh often used opposing colors such as purple and orange to add life to his paintings.

BED
CULTURE

BY NOW, MOST EVERYONE KNOWS that back in the eighteenth century, the bedroom was where high-level meetings took place—until Madame de Pompadour, the most famous of Louis XV's mistresses—removed her *chambre* from the list of public rooms. Gathering the trappings of an enviable lifestyle around her, she announced that privacy was the ultimate luxury. Then, in a quiet revolution, she boldly sealed her quarters from uninvited glares. Nothing suggested that the protocol she set in place would forever alter Gallic bedroom culture, yet all of France followed her example.

Nowadays, etiquette dictates that a bedroom door must remain shut both day and night. Also, it is poor manners for a person to peer into another person's *chambre*, whether or not someone is in the room. Almost always, the French close the shutters adorning their homes at night, much like Americans might hang a sign on the door requesting "Privacy." It is also unheard of to purchase a bedroom suite with wood finishes boringly alike.

No different from the time of the ancient Egyptians, eighteenth-century beds were the ultimate symbol of wealth. As a result, rivalry

Sleeping quarters have come a long way since the Middle Ages, when the occupants of a manor house slept together in the great hall with nary a thought. Until the eighteenth century, most homes did not have bedrooms. Instead, beds were moved from room to room, with velvet bed hangings offering privacy in aristocratic domains. Hand-painted bed by Patina wears fabric from the Ardecora Collection for Zimmer + Rohde. Bench is old. Area rug is from Stark Carpet. Royal-Pedic mattress befits one born to the manor or not. Perhaps prompted by Napoléon, who felt bigger is better, the U.S. bedding industry introduced the king-sized mattress in the mid-1950s.

for matchless levels of splendor fueled an array of variations. As befitting a majestic mansion, Madame de Pompadour and Louis XV's love swirled in a *lit à française* (canopied bed) with a crown presiding overhead. Opulent bed hangings billowed romantically, creating a luxurious room within a room when untied.

A door hanging brings a hotel sensibility into a home bent on guaranteeing a treasured guest a good night's sleep.

To this day, the French lavish extraordinary attention on their beds. For them, there are no hard-and-fast rules for bed linens to qualify as sensual, but the most elegant ones do share some common qualities that set them apart. Most all sheets are white or ecru and posh Egyptian cotton, if not 100 percent linen, which becomes softer and chalkier with age. Not hampered by thread count, which people say can be misleading beyond a soft 240 threads per square inch, there is awareness of the comfort bedding offers and the amenities of splendor: embroidery, appliqué and applied laces. Those not inclined to compromise their standards covet long, thin, single-ply fibers for extra softness and durability as well as pillowcases with an interior flap that not only hides the pillow from view but also helps keep it in place.

France has its own artfully layered bed culture that goes against the natural order of things, paying the rest of Europe little mind. Apart from what one sees, a stuffed and quilted mattress pad tops the mattress, followed by two flat sheets, then a blanket covered by another sheet. During the coolest months, a *couette* (duvet) filled with down that comes from the underbellies of geese (eiderdown fill is ultra light and the priciest) traps the warmth. Come morning, the French fold *les couettes* at the foot of the bed.

In the French mind, a bed is not complete without *un traversin*—a bolster, long and firm, spanning the mattress's width. Often it is wrapped in a blanket cover; always it supports European square pillows. Meanwhile, the top sheet—the middle sheet—generously turned back reveals a monogram or the family crest so that a person standing at the foot of the bed can read it readily.

By the mid-sixteenth century, the taste for monogrammed table and bed linens reached royal residences and then added a layer of respectability to dwellings beyond. Fancy or not, personalized linens were an extension of oneself, much like a signature deliberately crafted reinforces a

ABOVE: Pillow talk will never go out of style, so why not let a boudoir pillow with "good night" embroidered in numerous languages add a whimsical note? Beautiful linens were central to a noblewoman's dowry in sixteenth-century France.

OVERLEAF: A room with a view offers an inviting place to lounge other than the bed. With respect for the past, a modern version of seating otherwise known as récamier offers a tranquil spot to simply talk or to recharge with a good book. Fabric is from Jim Thompson. On windows: Ardecora for Zimmer+Rohde.

stylish image, for each letter formed part of the next, as if intent on making a lasting impression by remaining forever intertwined. Still, Diane de Poitiers, mistress of Henri II (1519–59), somehow managed to alter the official monogram of the French king and his queen, Catherine de Medici (1519–89), changing the intertwined H and C to H and D.

Today, monograms are no longer the domain of the rich and noble, of course. But they are regal indulgences adding to the price of beautiful linens. Across Europe, people begin assembling tabletop and bed linens for a baby girl's *trousseau* the moment she is born. Tradition dictates that the first letter of her given name reign on the left and the first letter of her surname on the right. The center awaits the first letter of her future husband's family name.

These days, a boudoir is as likely to serve as a spot for corresponding as for sleeping, so it typically includes a writing table. And, though area rugs often grace spaces, bare floors are common, too. Seldom do the French lay carpet. What's more, closets are rare. In fact, some say that armoires owe their enduring esteem to satisfying the need for storage space in rooms.

FACING: Malabar fabrics play off the blues in the nearby Gulf of Mexico, bringing coastal cool to a bedroom that awaits a fitting tenant: a young boy who loves visiting his grandparents. Dallas cabinetmaker Thomas Love crafted the walnut nightstands, which have handsome leather pulls. A narrow strip of fabric runs horizontally along the bottom edge of each Roman shade, increasing the window treatment's presence. ABOVE LEFT: Hand-hammered nail heads applied to a Samuel & Sons tape define a headboard with a sporty aesthetic that is as appropriate for today as for tomorrow. Shades trimmed in leather contribute to the distinctiveness of Ralph Lauren's leather-wrapped lamps. ABOVE RIGHT: Narrow roping gives a bed skirt crafted by Straight Stitch, Dallas, nautical flair while adding a layer of interest. Area rug is from Stark Carpet.

FACING: Resort comfort and splashes of Maria Flora's saturated blue 100 percent solution-dyed acrylic surround a see-worthy fire pit, anchored with the ambience of the French islands, where life moves at a slower pace. ABOVE: When it comes to hot chocolate, thicker is better, Europeans say, though it is not clear who first had the idea of warming it up. What is known: in the seventeenth-century, Louis XIII's wife, Anne of Austria, brought her love of chocolate to the royal court. Following her predecessor's example, Marie-Thérèse's passion for chocolate prompted her husband, Louis XIV, to install a "Royal Chocolate Maker to the King." Marie Antoinette's *specialist de chocolat* mixed the flavoring with powdered orchid bulbs or orange blossoms for her breakfast. Nevertheless, s'mores—short for "some mores"—are the ultimate fire pit accessory. Directions for making them first appeared in the 1927 *Girl Scout Handbook*.

On both sides of the ocean, outdoor living goes hand in hand with summer's relaxed mood. Whereas wine has long been the drink of choice in France, a mini-revolution has given rise to beer bar openings in the City of Light, leading to the coinage of *bièrologues*, or "beer sommeliers." In 1789, France's National Assembly legalized selling coffee, wine and spirits in the same place. **FACING:** Standing out at the pool: chairs that host a diverse group of crowd-pleasing cocktail recipes that have withstood the test of time. (All work as "mocktails," or alcohol-free offerings, as well.) Sand and starfish add interest to the vessel from Bergdorf Goodman, giving the setting a further edge.

OVERLEAF: Taking inspiration from the French Riviera, where blue is the prevailing hue and Cannes is one of the Mediterranean coastline's most famous resorts, a stateside family builds on the colors of the sea with umbrellas from Santa Barbara Designs and furniture awash in a Maria Flora solid and Giati stripe. In Louis XV's bedchamber, the royal coat of arms adorned the dressing screen, also known as a recess screen, as did palm trees.

DETAILS

IN THE SEVENTEENTH CENTURY, Louis XIV and his visionary finance minister, Jean-Baptist Colbert, established a strictly controlled guild system that regulated the work of artisans, raising the specialties at which they excelled to even higher standards. More than three centuries later, the Sun King perfectionism remains his extraordinary gift to France, though his penchant for opulence may be better known.

While the latter legacy may forever endure, King Louis XIV deserves credit for influencing most everything the French do. From their insistence on finely crafted furniture and regal textiles to turning out rooms with dignity and panache, the French attention to the detail, which borders on obsession, is testimony to the late king's fastidiousness and in keeping with his foresight.

In truth, the French leave no creative idea unimplemented, in hopes of making their living quarters special. Whether selecting quality leather for a chair or replacing door hardware, the attention to minutiae is striking.

In a nod to the classic trellises favored by the French, breakfast room chair pads enveloped in John Robshaw fabric ring a Portuguese dining table from Michael Taylor. Window treatment stripe is by Ralph Lauren, who comes close to having the cultural impact that the French exert.

Finely etched knobs, surface bolts and crémone bolts that could almost pass for artwork bestow added nobility on groaning doors and tall, narrow windows. Crisp crown moldings, seamlessly woven, step out onto ceilings, making spaces appear even taller than they actually are. Polished brass grilles with scrolled motifs adorn heating vents, elevating the ordinary.

Whereas small paintings would disappear on generous walls, grouped with mirrors and wall sconces, they make a strong statement. Meanwhile, heroic-sized family portraits add splendor and historic character.

Further suggesting the sophistication of a former era, several rock-crystal chandeliers may drift overhead in the same room. While shaded sconces wash walls with light, picture lights cast a soft glow, and table and floor lamps direct glare. Together they maneuver light into producing drama and warmth not attainable with overhead sources. Generally, the French shy away from track lighting, which can jarringly cast unforgiving shadows on the face.

Attention to detail glorifies the image of the Sun King, whose influence is still felt these hundreds of years later.

In their kitchens, perhaps, but elsewhere the French aren't champions of a cluttered look, or small-scale antiques.

PREVIOUS OVERLEAF: Building on the homeowner's love of blue in all its myriad hues, a new construction defines itself with noticeable French flair and some decidedly modern twists. Sofa fabric is from Rogers & Goffigon; Romo covers the field bench. (The quilted leather Chanel handbag in deep blue began life in Alsace, in an old stone building.) Residing on a sofa table from Jacqueline Adams Antiques, Atlanta, is a pair of lamps with pleated shades by Cele Johnson, Dallas, and classic blue-and-white porcelain, varying in age, collected over time.

FACING ABOVE: Dime-sized mirrors imbue an inky blue, intricately embroidered, hand-blocked John Robshaw print—inspired by the textile designer's trip to the plains of Rajasthan, India—with an air of glamour, while a fringed cashmere Ralph Lauren throw bearing an embroidered street name graces the sofa. FACING BELOW: When a narrow tape darts across a chair skirt, the result is eye-catching. Tape is from Samuel & Sons; fabric by Quadrille; area rug is Stark. ABOVE: No bedroom is complete without flowers, and artfully clipped leaves can set an arrangement apart.

FACING: At small, informal get-togethers, the French often serve in the library, sitting room or even the kitchen, reserving the dining room for larger, regal affairs. In this case, an area just steps from the bar also works for wine tastings. Chairs fashionably dressed in Cowtan & Tout surround a walnut table—crafted in France—which rests on imposing marble floors. Double-walled blown glass filled with liquid silver—better known today as mercury glass—was first produced in Bohemia, now the Czech Republic, in the mid-nineteenth century. ABOVE: Wet bars today have come up from the basement, which is not to say all are equally grand. Being conveniently sited steps from the dining area makes this the perfect gathering spot for pre-dinner conversations, cocktails and hors d'oeuvres.

White, dove and café au lait join forces to emit a sophisticated, gracious air in a villa that exudes more than a bit of contemporary glamour. A vintage bar cart rests between chairs in the style of Louis XVI, wearing Clarke & Clarke. Tall, narrow vase is by Baccarat, as are the votives. Area rug from Stark Carpet graces marble floors. The ottoman of today is only vaguely reminiscent of the long, backless settee from which the privileged sultan of the vast Ottoman Empire ruled during the fourteenth century.

FACING: A setting where "less is more" mingles eras and styles. Traditionally, the French gravitate to lamps 27 to 30 inches tall. Those taller exude a modern sensibility and fittingly wear drum shades. The rock crystal tiered lamp produced in London for Chameleon Fine Lighting, New York, sits on a resplendent eighteenth-century walnut commode from Jacqueline Adams Antiques, Atlanta, as does its (unseen) sister, flanking the other side of the fireplace. Philippe II mirrors add depth to the room rather than reflecting the vanity of society, as the pair once undoubtedly did. Until about 1875, mirrors were called looking glasses. ABOVE: Pillows touting *passementerie* from the French house of Houlès prop on channel-backed sofas clad in Christopher Hyland's luxuriously textured "Kimmel."

While the French tend to shun most anything that has potential for spawning envy, Americans often take a different tack. On this side of the Atlantic, there's no shame in spoiling ourselves in private home theaters with 3D TV and surround sound, anymore than 150-foot yachts or traveling the world. FACING: No trip to the movie theater is complete without a stop at the concession stand. Theater-style seating with cup holders is available from Marroquin Upholstery.

AFTERWORD

AFTER CENTURIES OF GILT FURNITURE that screams for attention, the French are beyond that. But, then, rarely do we stay true to one king. Regardless of on which side of the Atlantic one resides, it has become de rigueur to fluidly layer the past and present, mixing clean-lined, mid-century modern furnishings with period furniture and, yes, embrace the look of unassuming luxury that is right for today.

For us, interior decorating has become both art and science, a passion and, indeed, a pleasurable pursuit revealing our individual visions if not chronicling our travels and divulging our interests. Admittedly, we draw upon those fundamentals firmly fixed in our minds to shape settings warm, comfortable and inviting. For these, we thank our design ally, the French, and their ever-so-chic way of expressing both beauty and taste.

Smitten with his own reflection, Louis XIV decreed the construction of the Hall of Mirrors in 1678, elevating the looking glass to the most sought-after symbol of splendor. Here, an outsized Nancy Corzine mirror hovers over the console, while instantly identifiable prints from the House of Chanel bring unexpected dash to a foyer with space constraints. Separating lanterns from Baccarat, the celebrated French crystal company, is an elongated vessel laden with bold French hydrangeas— or *hortensia*, as the French call them—with blooms ranging in depth from white to pale blue and leaves trimmed below the water line; by Tom Trovato for Grace Lake's Florist, Naples, Florida.

CREDITS

DESIGN DIRECTORY

ALINE ALPHEN

Aline Alphen

72 Chemin des Hautes Royères

84440 Robion, France

Office: 33 638 686 371

www.alinealphen.com

BETTY LOU PHILLIPS, ASID

Interiors by BLP

4200 St. Johns Drive

Dallas, Texas 75205

Studio: 214.599.0191

www.Bettylouphillips.com

PAMELA PIERCE

Pam Pierce Designs

2422 Bartlett, Suite 5

Houston, Texas 77098

Office: 713.961.7540

www.ppiercedesigns.com

NICOLE DOMERCQ ZARR

Triangle Interiors, Inc.

1513 West Dallas Street

Houston, Texas 77098

Office: 713.973.6040

www.Triangleinteriors.com

Drawing on his fashion sense, an artist in the walled hilltop village of Ménerbes offers unassuming hand-painted chair covers in multiple styles. Ménerbes is in the foothills of the French Alps.

DESIGNER CREDITS

Aline Alphen: Copyright page, 6, 18–19, 22, 24–25, 26, 28–29, 30–31, 32, 33, 34–35, 36, 37, 38–39, 40, 41, 42, 43, 44, 45, 46–47, 48–49, 50–51, 52, 53, 54, 55, 56, 57, 58, 59, 60, 61, 62–63, 84–85, 86, 87, 88, 89, 90, 92, 93, 94, 95, 96, 97, 98, 99, 100, 101, 102, 103, 204–05, 227.

Betty Lou Phillips: 6, 7, 13, 17, 104–05, 106–07, 108, 109, 111, 112, 113, 114–15, 116, 117, 118–19, 120–21, 122, 123, 124, 128–29, 131, 132–33, 134, 135, 136, 137, 138, 139, 140, 141, 142, 144, 146–47, 148, 149, 150, 151, 152, 153, 154, 155, 206–07, 208, 209, 210–11, 212, 213, 214, 215, 216, 217, 218–19, 220–21, 222–23, 224–25, 226, 228, 229, 230–31, 232–33, 234, 235, 236–37.

Pamela Pierce: 6, 64, 69, 70, 71, 72, 73, 74–75, 76, 77.

Nicole Zarr: Front Cover, Back Cover, 6, 7, 8, 156–57, 159, 160, 162–63, 164–65, 166–67, 168, 169, 170–71, 172, 173, 175, 176–77, 178, 179, 180–81, 182–83, 194–95, 196, 197, 198–99, 200–01, 202, 203.

PHOTOGRAPHY CREDITS

Dan Piassick: Front Cover, Back Cover, all pages except:

Betty Lou Phillips: 7, 11, 14, 20, 66, 109, 185, 186, 193, 238.

Amy Werntz: Title page, 12, 21, 109, 145.

Petit Photography: Author's Photograph.

The old, the unusual and the unexpected seldom fail to capture the interest of interior designers. Together these components led to the creation of a small but stylish powder room with worldly appeal, thanks to Chateau Domingue champion of *éléments* (artisanal stone, tile, fireplaces and more) French and Italian.